THE FATHERHOOD FRAMEWORK

A journey with a purpose

THE FATHERHOOD FRAMEWORK

A journey with a purpose

CLAYTON TUMMONS

The Fatherhood Framework

Copyright © 2022 Clayton Tummons

All rights reserved. No part of this book may be reproduced in any form or by any electronic or mechanical means, including information storage and retrieval systems, without written permission from the author, except for the use of brief quotations in a book review.

All scripture is from the ESV translation unless otherwise noted. Scripture quotations are from the ESV® Bible (The Holy Bible, English Standard Version®), copyright © 2001 by Crossway, a publishing ministry of Good News Publishers. Used by permission. All rights reserved.

Scriptures taken from the Holy Bible, New International Version®, NIV®. Copyright © 1973, 1978, 1984, 2011 by Biblica, Inc.™ Used by permission of Zondervan. All rights reserved worldwide. www.zondervan.com The "NIV" and "New International Version" are trademarks registered in the United States Patent and Trademark Office by Biblica, Inc.™

Scripture quotations marked (KJV) are taken from the King James Version.

Cover Design: John Posey

ISBN 979-8-9872974-0-7 (Paperback)

ISBN 979-8-9872974-1-4 (Hardcover)

ISBN 979-8-9872974-2-1 (eBook)

Learn more at www.claytontummons.com

To Titus and Kate,
I love being your father.

CONTENTS

Introduction	9
1. What is a Father?	17
2. The Old Man	43
3. A Father Loves	67
4. A Father Provides	81
5. A Father Protects	95
6. A Father Forgives	109
7. A Father Serves	121
8. A Father Helps	131
9. A Father Prays	141
10. A Father Teaches	151
11. A Father Disciplines	161
12. A Father Gives	171
13. Knowing the Father	179
14. The Framework	187
Thank You	195
Share This Book	197
Family Plan	199
Study Guide	201
About the Author	203
Notes	205
Prayer List	207

INTRODUCTION

I'm glad you're here. Maybe you've been given this book by a friend or family member, or perhaps you even purchased it for yourself. Regardless of how you ended up reading this, I commend you on your desire to grow as a father. I believe this desire is needed more today than ever before.

Why are you here? Take a moment to think about this question. Why are you reading this book? You could be doing hundreds of other things with your time, but right now, you're sitting somewhere holding this book in your hands. Maybe you've decided you may not have everything figured out as a father and you're wanting to learn more.

I admire your desire to become a better father. This is a desire I share myself. The fact you're thinking along these lines shows your interest in tackling one of the most challenging responsibilities given to many of us in life. What are your desires for being a father? Where do you feel like you're not quite prepared? What keeps you up at night or bothers you at the end of the day? What areas of growth would you like to see in your fatherhood journey?

These are all deep questions I want you to think about before we move any further. Let me ask you again – why are you here reading this book? Don't just answer with "I want to be a better father," because hopefully, that's a given. I believe most fathers want to be good fathers. If wanting to be a good father was all it took, we would already be good fathers. It takes something more than just desire. Be specific, what do you want to work on in your fatherhood journey?

Maybe your kids are navigating their teenage years and boys are starting to show up at your house to see your daughter. If this is you, you might want to gain wisdom to navigate the dating years and learn how to guard your daughter's heart during these life-changing times.

Perhaps your children are little, and you're unsure how to direct them as they grow up. You might have questions like, "How do I teach them about the Bible?" or "How can I make sure they have good friends surrounding them?" I can assure you these are questions many fathers struggle with, so don't feel alone.

You might have one child, or you might have many. Some of your fears might be financially supporting them as they grow up or teaching your children about the world around them. How will you navigate the changing culture which pulls for their attention every day? You may feel scared or unequipped to deal with the needs of a growing family, or you might even be a single dad trying to figure all of this father stuff out on your own.

What about God? How will you teach your children about the creator of the universe? Do you have a plan in place to shepherd your kids and wife? If your children are grown, what truths in scripture are you teaching them as they navigate their own parenting? Use this time to think about why you're here to learn about fatherhood. Just know, other fathers are either right where you are or have been there themselves in the past. We're going to go through this journey together.

As you read this book, I encourage you to make notes, circle things, highlight areas you want to remember and be open with your thoughts and challenges as we discover what true fatherhood looks like in the following pages. The only way we're going to be able to make a change and work towards being better fathers is to start with deep internal reflection. Take a moment right now to ponder these questions and think about why you're here. Take all the time you need. It's worth it.

I'm writing this book because I'm on this fatherhood journey too. Let me start by saying, I'm not perfect. Not even close. My daily failings are vast and I typically feel quite inadequate in being not only a father but a husband too. I don't have all the answers and I haven't experienced all the phases of life. However, I'm certain of one thing. I don't want to look back on my life as a father as someone who didn't point his family to a greater purpose.

There are times when I'm not present or I'm tired after a

long day of work, but I believe being a father is one of the most rewarding callings in life. How do we navigate this journey? How will you or I know what we should do or when we should do it? Who will show us? Each day comes only once. Whatever date it is today as you're reading this book, you'll only get this exact day one time, then it's gone. There may be another "October 5th" (the date I'm writing this) but you won't get another October 5th of this year ever again.

Each day happens only once. There might be more days ahead but each one is special in its own right because it's like a new page in a book. It's almost as if an invisible author is writing down each day for us in the form of memories. Our current actions quickly translate into stories of the past. Over time, these shape those around us. Today, what will be written on the page of your life as a father?

This book is written for all fathers, not just the ones in my current phase of life. Whether you're a biological father, stepfather, adoptive father, foster father, father-in-law, single father, or even just a father figure, I know you'll be able to gain insight into whatever stage of life you're in. Whether your children are still little or grown with kids of their own, I believe you can learn and see how God's design for fatherhood will meet you right where you are.

You might even be reading this book as a future father with your first child on the way. If this is you, congratulations on the journey you're about to start. Many have gone before you and if we learn about fatherhood and equip ourselves with the right purpose, this expedition will not be in vain. You might even be reading this book with the desire to simply be a father someday.

Perhaps you're even a grandfather. You likely have more wisdom than most and can be a resource to younger fathers around you. You've experienced more of life and have great stories to tell about how the world has changed as you've grown older. You'll be able to share where you think you got this fatherhood journey right, and where you didn't. I always enjoy sitting with wiser, older men who can pour into me and share their knowledge on how they navigated fatherhood throughout their life.

Why did I call this book "The Fatherhood Framework"? It's a framework for fatherhood based on God's demonstration of fatherhood to us. Thankfully, we don't have to guess what a good father looks like. We can open his word to see throughout the Bible how a perfect father loves and cares for his children. Some of you might have a goal of being a good father. There is nothing wrong with a goal but a goal doesn't show you how to do something – it's only the hopeful result. We want to view and understand a framework in which we can prayerfully ask God to help us follow his design of fatherhood as we seek to become good fathers.

Throughout this book, I'm going to reference the Bible to discuss how I believe God has given us the ultimate picture of the fatherhood framework. His picture for fatherhood will not fail us because he hasn't failed us. If we have to rely on ourselves to get this fatherhood journey right, we're doomed. However, if we seek God and understand the bigger picture of fatherhood displayed to us throughout scripture, we'll not only succeed at the task but we'll have the best seat in the house to watch God's glory unfold in the lives of our children.

Maybe you've been going to church your whole life or just recently started learning about God. Perhaps you're a new believer who is excited to continue living the life only God can give you. If you've been a follower of Jesus most of your life, you might feel like you've missed some key elements to the fatherhood journey and don't quite know where to start. Perhaps you've read a lot of the Bible or very little.

You might even be someone reading this book who doesn't believe in God at all. If this is you, I encourage you to hang in there and listen to the material ahead. Compare it to your current plan as a father to see where you can improve. If you apply these truths to your life, I know you'll find a better way to father your children and lead your household. It doesn't matter your past. What matters is how you will choose to spend your future as a father. If the content ahead speaks to you in a personal way, there is a chapter near the end to give you more information on who God is and how you can know him personally.

Again, I'm so glad you're here and I'm looking forward to what God is going to do with you while reading this book. I'm praying for you and your journey with fatherhood. I encourage you to read this book in its entirety. Use the material here to help shape your prayers as a father. Ask God to reveal to you where you can improve, and always lean on him. As you'll see as we move forward, he's the perfect father so just know you already have the best teacher who will be with you every step of the way.

There are so many activities in the world that take your time and energy each day. It's a blessing to be a father and invest in the lives of our children. They are truly a gift. Life moves fast and they're only under our roof for a short time. I encourage you in the pages ahead to self-reflect and be ready to go to work. Look deep within and don't leave anything off the table. It's just too important. Let's get after it.

1

WHAT IS A FATHER?

I don't think there has been anything more life-changing in the context of our present world for me than becoming a father. This has brought more joy and fear than anything else I've experienced. I'll never forget the night my wife Amy told me she thought she might be pregnant. To be fair, we had been trying for a short time but could it be true? Naturally in our modern world of conveniences, we didn't have to wonder for long as she promptly went back to our bathroom to take a pregnancy test.

What I think was about 10 minutes seemed like an eternity, and waiting in the kitchen together for the results was needless to say, a bit challenging. I'm not the most patient person. I'm a show-up-early kind of guy. I relish in details and order so I'm mentally analyzing every second that goes by waiting for the test to be complete. Finally, the moment of truth has come. We both walk quietly into the bathroom and peer over the vanity to see the results. Two lines. We're pregnant. At this moment our lives have changed forever. I'm immediately overjoyed and terrified. You might relate to this feeling if you've been in the same situation as me.

At the time of writing this book, I have a four-year-old boy named Titus and an almost two-year-old girl named Kate. They are both amazing children. At our house, you'll currently find superheroes and baby dolls scattered all around. Life is busy. The days are long, but at the same time, very short. Over the last few years, my wife Amy and I have been on the ride of our lives. Whether it's changing diapers, navigating all the firsts like walking, talking, using a fork, potty training, or even driving 12 hours with two little ones on our first family beach trip, we're learning to tackle it all.

Maybe right now you're in the same season as me or maybe these days are long behind you. Regardless of which season you're in today, I think you can relate to the chaos of life in all its glory. Some days seem like they'll never come to a close and others have you wanting more time together.

If you're a father who is in the midst of little children like myself, or if your children are grown up, take a moment to pray and thank God for the blessing of being a father. The Bible tells us children are a heritage (gift) from the Lord. I think anyone with children would agree. "Behold, children are a heritage from the LORD, the fruit of the womb a reward" (Psalm 127:3).

Do you remember the "choose your own adventure" books growing up? The idea behind these books was the reader could pick a path and the story would end differently based on what decisions you made along the way. If you wanted to go into the enchanted forest you might discover a castle and end up becoming a knight. If you instead decided to go through the desert, you might end up discovering riches in a faraway land. You would encounter everything from adventures to various trials. However, the end of the story was always a result of your own decisions. If you finished with an ending you didn't like, you had no one to blame but yourself.

While these books aren't real, they are a lot like fatherhood. As a father, you'll have the opportunity to make decisions as you raise your children. You can choose to be an active father or a passive one throughout your life. You can teach your children or you can let the world teach them. Just like in these books, the end of your story will be up to you.

DEFINING A FATHER

What is a father? It may seem pretty obvious but take a moment to think about how you would answer this question. I imagine you would say something like, "A father is someone who has children of their own." This may be oversimplified but is otherwise correct. The definition of a father is easy but the role of being a father is hard. So what would you say is the role of a father? Your role as a father is to watch over and raise your children. This is a role you'll have for life and it's a role where you have a choice. What kind of father will you choose to be?

I know if you've been a father for any amount of time you've come to realize there are almost no days where you feel completely qualified in your role. It feels at best like you miss most shots you take and once in a while you do something which feels close to right but the moment passes quickly without much celebration. At least this is how I feel in my own life most days.

Life goes by in a hurry. Everyone and everything is continuously moving around you. Your children's birthdays seem to come quicker each year and you feel as if you just celebrated one when another is right around the corner. I recently heard a statement in which life is like a roll of toilet paper. The closer you get to the end the faster it goes. I wish I could take credit for this profound revelation, but alas, someone out there is the victor on this one.

With life flying by you, how will you establish a plan for making sure you're raising your children well? What will you use as the standard to base your own fatherhood decisions? How will you model true fatherhood over the years as they grow up? How are you going to teach them about God? What about the Bible? What about how to pray? How are you going to shepherd them when someone in your family passes away? What steps do you have in place today which are leading them closer to Jesus? Are you reading them the Bible when they're young so they'll desire to read it on their own as they get older?

Maybe you only have little kids at the moment and aren't too worried about all of this just yet. Remember by the time you "remember" to start being a father, they'll be well on their way to being shaped by someone other than you. Fathers, it's not your church's responsibility to raise your children, it's not their school's responsibility, or anyone else for that matter – it's yours.

If you think they're going to be model students who turn

into model adults because you shuttled them to church on Sunday mornings, you're in for a rude awakening. I'll save you the trouble right now. If you happened to grow up a "church kid" then you might remember some fellow youth group students who attended quite often and ended up in a world of hurt later on in life. You might have been someone who veered off the path for a season yourself. We've all heard the stereotype of a "pastor's kid" and sometimes it's true.

Fatherhood isn't just for dads with little kids. What if your children are grown with children of their own? How will you continue to shepherd them? Your role as a father isn't over just because they no longer live in your home. They will look to you for guidance but are you ready to help? If you're a grandfather, your role continues with the next generation.

If you're a father, there's a good chance you're married, too. What about your wife? Are you spending time with her? Do your children see how much you love her? Every wife is also someone's daughter, you know. If you have a daughter, think about how you would want a husband to treat her. Our daughter Kate is the sweetest little girl I know. My wife Amy is the "Kate" to another father in the world and this perspective helps remind me to continually work on our relationship, too.

I think you're starting to see how important your job as a father is going to be. Your children want a father to love and teach them. They will need your help throughout life. Above all, they need you to point them to Jesus. No one wants to grow up without a father pouring into them. Your children will grow up, with or without you, and you can't do anything about it.

Here's a crucial detail in this fatherhood journey – there is a perfect father out there, but it's not you.

FATHERHOOD STATISTICS

What's at stake? What are the consequences of a weak fatherhood culture within our society? What might happen to your children if you don't own this fatherhood journey? The ramifications of a lack of biblical fatherhood are tremendous. Absent fathers who aren't involved in the lives of their children are like a virus that spreads to the next generation. This self-replicating epidemic cannot be contained but permeates throughout the world. It seemingly goes undetected as it spreads but its effects are devastating.

Children learn what fatherhood looks like from their father, whether it's good or bad. You don't have to be an absent father for your children to be a victim of this problem. You can be a fully present father physically, but absent in other ways. For example, being a distracted father with work or other areas of your life can be just as catastrophic.

Perhaps you're a father who has a strained relationship with your children. If there is family tension from the past, how will you rebuild relationships which may be broken? Do you want to waste another day with the feelings of separation or do you want to seek restoration and begin building a life together again? No matter the circumstances or the scars of the past, you can work to restore relationships that have been sidelined for too long. It may not be easy and will likely require you to make some changes, but the outcome is possible and it starts with you.

The change we need must start with fathers who display God's design for fatherhood first in their own homes. We have to treat the problem at the source. It has to start now and it has to start with you. You have to lead your household in reflecting God's design for fatherhood if you want your children to have any hope of surviving the world around them.

Beyond the basic idea of populating the earth, why is fatherhood so important? What would happen in the world if fathers started taking their role more seriously? I believe fatherhood can not only shape the direction of our households but proper fatherhood points our children and others to Jesus.

We are surrounded by a culture where fatherhood has become passive and weak. This allows for several problems, not only on earth, but ones with eternal consequences. Our society lacks men with convictions who fear God and teach their children to do the same. This leads to children raising children, and who would ever think that's a good idea?

A FATHERLESS GENERATION

Take a look at the following statistics to see where a lack of fatherhood in our society has brought us:

- 1 in 4 children live in a home without a dad.[1]
- Fatherless children are at a dramatically greater risk of drug and alcohol abuse.[2]

- Men who live with absent fathers are more likely to become absent fathers themselves. (Remember our analogy above on how a virus self-replicates? Here's proof.)[3]
- A Department of Justice survey of 7,000 inmates revealed that 39% of jail inmates lived in mother-only households.[4]

I think you can see just some of what's at stake if we don't take fatherhood seriously. These are only a handful of the shocking statistics in a society with a lack of fatherhood. Will you be a father who says enough is enough? Will you choose to say "Not today" and "Not in my house"? Will you be the father God designed you to be?

A CULTURAL SHIFT

Children today are facing more challenges than any other generation in history. Without fathers helping them navigate these difficult times, you're not only leaving them in a battle without any armor, but you're leading them right into it. It's like walking a baby deer into a pack of hungry wolves. Unfortunately, the deer in this scenario is your child.

With the complexity of the issues surrounding us and the growing worldly desire to suppress biblical truth, without true fatherhood, how will any of our children succeed? How will they know what to do when they see children at their school with gender identity issues? What about homosexuality? Who will teach them about God's design for marriage? Who will be the first person to explain sex or teach them about the harmful effects of porn? These are complex issues that need to be navigated by their father.

Your children will discover all of the above and more. Probably at an age that will make you cringe. The question is, who will be the one teaching them? Will it be you or will it be the world? Their peers will be happy to "educate" them on what is "right" if you won't. This is scary stuff.

These are just some of the more common issues our society is dealing with today but we all know there is an even longer list of life events that need direction from a father, too. These events are circumstances almost all children will face at some point in their life. Who will teach your son how to properly treat a girl when he starts dating? Who will tell your daughter how she was made in the image of God and guard her heart against sex outside of marriage? Who will cheer them through all the ups and downs of life? Fathers, this must be you.

WHO IS YOUR FATHER?

Who was your father? Did you even know him? There are so many different situations in which you might have been raised. You might have had a father in your home growing up or you might not have. Perhaps your mother or a grandparent, aunt, or uncle has been the father figure in your life since birth. You may know who your father is but he may have been absent during your childhood and teenage years. You might not even know who your father is at all.

While an absent father is very common in our society, you

don't have to repeat this situation in the lives of your children. If you did happen to grow up in a household where your father was absent, remember this important truth from the Bible. "Father of the fatherless and protector of widows is God in his holy habitation" (Psalm 68:5).

Our God is a father to the fatherless. If your earthly father was absent from your life, know this is not a picture of your Heavenly Father. Even before you were born, God loved you. In the book of Jeremiah, chapter 31 verse 3 says, "...I have loved you with an everlasting love." As we'll see in the chapters that follow, God's love is the foundation for all of his wonderful characteristics as a father.

Many men today struggle with their father and upbringing. This makes it much harder for them to be fathers themselves. They don't know what real fatherhood looks like because they didn't see it modeled to them growing up. They desire to be a good dad but they don't know what to do.

Take a moment and think about your father. What was he like? What are some good memories you have together? How did he impact your life? What did he do well? What could he have done better? If you were lucky enough to have a father who taught you about God and the sacrifice Jesus made for us on the cross, take a moment to thank God for your earthly father's leadership in your life. Pray for him and his relationship with God. Ask God to heal any areas of your relationship which may need repair.

All fathers share similar fears and insecurities. Many desire to be good fathers but remember, all fathers are sons, too. Yes, your dad is someone else's son and has both good and bad from their upbringing which has shaped who they are as fathers themselves. No earthly father is perfect, but loving your father is something you can do even if he wasn't around.

As you know, being a father is hard and while your father may have done well, he may not feel this way. Hearing from his son how he's shaped, encouraged, and helped you along the way would mean the world to him. Don't wait until his life's coming to a close. Let him know how much you love him and how thankful you are to have him in your life.

If your father has passed away. Take a moment to remember the good times you had and thank God for all the memories you were able to share. Our fathers seem invincible but we all know that given enough time, they won't be with us forever. Savor those memories and tell your children about your father. Tell them about his wonderful characteristics and stories from your childhood.

There are situations in life that are very difficult for sons to acknowledge their fathers. Many have experienced the abuse of a father growing up. Perhaps your father was an image of anger and displayed it physically to you or other family members. If this is similar to your situation, know this is not a reflection of the God of the Bible.

If you're struggling with the idea of showing love to someone abusive or absent from your life, know the idea of loving someone who hasn't been there for you is difficult but also remember this is how God first loved you. While we were sinners, broken, and living in a hopeless state, God loved us. "...But God shows his love for us in that while we were still sinners, Christ died for us" (Romans 5:8). God's love is not only for the righteous because none of us are righteous. "...As it is written: None is righteous, no, not one;" (Romans 3:10).

We know from scripture that everyone is a sinner and our entire world is fractured because of sin. God loved us when we didn't love him. While we were off seeking our selfish desires, God still loved us. We didn't have to get right before God started loving us and he loved us in all of our sinful nature.

Your father, his father, and also yourself are all sinners in need of a savior. If your father is still in a state of brokenness, work to follow God's example and love those who don't deserve it. Remember, while you were in a state of brokenness, God loved you.

THE PERFECT FATHER

As a father, do you ever feel like you've done something you wish you could take back? How about feeling like you're not sure how to discipline your children as they age? Do you ever think, "Was I too harsh?" Suffice it to say, you're not a perfect father and the reality is, you won't ever be. If you're striving for perfection, you're going to be disappointed with the results.

There is never a moment when I feel like I'm doing the role of a father as well as I'd like. At times, I find myself ruminating on something I could have done differently. I'm always aiming to do the right thing but I mess up and feel bad for failing my kids. These self-reflections may sound familiar to you, too.

If you were to think about a perfect father, how would you describe him? You might think of a father from a show growing up or even a father from a book. Perhaps it's the dad who never misses their child's sports game or someone who always has the right words to say in a tough moment. There are many examples of fatherhood but none of these examples would be a perfect father. There is no perfect earthly father. We all mess up because we're all sinful people. Our flesh pulls at us each day and we'll never hit the mark.

If you've put your faith in Jesus, you are part of God's family. You've been adopted through Jesus and made an heir with him (Romans 8:17). God has prepared for you a place at the table and you are welcomed into his presence whenever you call on his name. As a part of God's family, you are now the son of a perfect father. Yes, the God of the universe is the perfect father and you are his son. He's unchanging and will never fail you. He wants to show you how to be the father you want to be, too.

Throughout the New Testament, we see Jesus crying out to the father, calling on the father, and praying to the father. Why is this? Jesus knows he can do nothing without the father (John 5:19). This was true for him and it's true for you, too. We are no different. We are incapable of discerning right from wrong, leading our families to Jesus, or living a joyous life apart from him. Spend time reading Psalms and you'll see David pouring his heart out in reliance on God. He knows it's only God who can help him in his times of trouble, or God who can be praised for all his wondrous deeds. He knows God is his protector, provider, and helper.

Jesus refers to God in scripture as "Abba Father" but what does this mean? The word "Abba" is an Aramaic word that means "Father" that represents the ultimate fatherhood relationship. This term reflects a deeply personal one. It displays a father-and-child relationship that is held to the highest standard of trust. The term is only used three times in scripture by Jesus and the apostle Paul. It's a very sacred term.

One time when Jesus uses the term "Abba Father" is when he's praying in the Garden of Gethsemane right before he was going to be crucified. This was one of the toughest times Jesus was going to have to call on his father for help. Jesus knows in just a few hours, he's going to experience death and separation from God. He has to take the full weight of the sins of the world upon himself. He's so anxious that he literally sweats blood.

He asks his father to remove this cup but knows there is no other option. Jesus must go to the cross to crush the sins of the world. What he says at the end of his prayer is our opportunity to begin to know and trust a perfect father. Jesus says, "Yet not what I will, but what you will" (Mark 14:36). Jesus knows his father has his best interest at heart. He knows his father will not let him down because he never has. He knows to trust him. This is the same for us, too. You and I have a perfect Heavenly Father who desires for his children to follow him and reflect his design for fatherhood to our children.

We must look to our Heavenly Father as our model for fatherhood. There will be many times in your fatherhood journey when you won't know what to do or say. However, if we lean on him each day, he'll show us along the way.

WHAT IS A MAN?

What is a man? If you're a father, you're also a man. Thoughts of stereotypical "manly" things could be coming to mind. You might think of someone physically strong or someone with facial hair like a beard. What about someone who hunts or goes fishing? You might think of someone who fixes cars in the garage and works with his hands. While these may be descriptions of some men, not all men have these abilities or physical appearances. Therefore none of the above defines a man.

What does the Bible say about a man? If you look at the very beginning of the book of Genesis you can see how everything starts with God. In Genesis, God created the world and everything in it. "Then God said, 'Let us make man in our image, after our likeness. And let them have dominion over the fish of the sea and over the birds of the heavens and over the livestock and over all the earth and over every creeping thing that creeps on the earth'" (Genesis 1:26).

Right here in this passage, God created man. He created man in his image. Both men and women are God's most prized creations because we reflect his image. While there are amazing aspects of creation, nothing is more amazing than mankind. To properly define a man, we would say, "man is someone created in the image of God and designed to display who he is."

God created us with many characteristics. For example, we can be creative, caring, loving, and many other attributes just like him. We all have an inner sense of enjoyment to be a part of something bigger than ourselves and this design manifests itself throughout our lives in various ways. Some of these are life pursuits and passions. Some are the vocations we choose. All of these outlets reflect the characteristics of the original creator – God. As a man, God has designed you for some very specific roles. Let's learn about some of them now.

MADE TO WORK

Later on in Genesis, God said before creating man, there was no one to "work the ground." "When no bush of the field was yet in the land and no small plant of the field had yet sprung up —for the LORD God had not caused it to rain on the land, and there was no man to work the ground" (Genesis 2:5). God had created the most amazing place in the Garden of Eden with everything one would need. The garden had incredible animals, plants, food to eat, and water flowing throughout. It was paradise. However, it was missing someone to take care of it all.

Since there was no one to work the ground, God created man to take care of his creation. The Bible says, "...then the LORD God formed the man of dust from the ground and breathed into his nostrils the breath of life, and the man became a living creature" (Genesis 2:7). From the beginning, we were designed by God to work.

I want to touch on something briefly. We live in a culture where we too often try to find the quick and easy way to a life without work. This idea of "getting rich" quickly and not having to work is not in alignment with God's original design of man. You've just seen how God created you as a man to work, so while there are some hard days, working is a way you can worship God. I just wanted you to know God originally designed man to work his creation, and while you might not be tending the Garden of Eden 40 hours a week, you can worship the creator in whatever you do. As it says in scripture, "So, whether you eat or drink, or whatever you do, do all to the glory of God" (1 Corinthians 10:31).

So far we've learned how we were created in the image of God. We also learned how God designed us to work his creation. Now let's take a look at responsibility. Who are we responsible for? We read in the previous passages how man was responsible for working the garden but are there other responsibilities for which God designed man uniquely?

THE ROLE OF A HUSBAND

If you're a father, there is a good chance that you're a husband, too. To understand fatherhood and all which comes with it, we need to understand God's design for marriage. Our role as a man within this design is unlike anything else. Marriage was created and established by God. Let's look at the book of Genesis to see how this unfolded. "Then the LORD God said, 'It is not good that the man should be alone; I will make him a helper fit for him'" (Genesis 2:18).

God created everything, this includes both men and women. He created them uniquely to serve different roles in his creation. Marriage is a partnership. Each role has different functions but they both are created by God. Our wives are a blessing and if you're lucky enough to be married to an amazing woman, take a moment right now to thank God for her and the gift of marriage. I know in my own life, my wife Amy takes care of our household like Superwoman and I wouldn't want to do life without her. Our children love her and I do, too.

Later in verse 24, God establishes the picture of marriage in scripture, "Therefore a man shall leave his father and his mother and hold fast to his wife, and they shall become one flesh" (Genesis 2:24). God has given us a design in which the husband and wife can come alongside their children to help point them to him.

Marriage is a sacred union because it's a visual representation of Christ and the church. A husband's responsibility is to sacrificially lay down his life for his wife as Christ laid down his life for the church when he died on the cross. The husband represents Christ and the wife represents his church.

It's incredible to think about how all married people walking around are a visible representation of this biblical picture. Anytime we see two married people together, we should immediately think of Christ and the church. Seriously, anytime we go to a wedding, Christ and the church. Anytime you see a married couple grocery shopping together, Christ and the church. If you pass a husband and wife jogging while you're driving to work, again, Christ and the church. Pretty amazing, right? How is it we just see "married" people in these moments instead of the bigger picture God has created for us?

Do you remember the "slug bug" game you played in the car growing up? Anytime you saw a Volkswagen you would hit the person sitting next to you and say "slug bug!" I encourage you to start a new game with your spouse in which you start pointing out all the married couples you see while you're out and about. Lightly nudge the other person and say "Christ and the church." This might get a laugh but it will help you remember the real picture of marriage and its meaning.

Why is this picture meaningful? It's meaningful because it demonstrates the ultimate sacrifice of what God has done for all of us through Jesus. His death and resurrection were the only way we could have a relationship with him. Marriage is ultimately a picture of the Gospel.

Another way it's meaningful is for others to see. If we all viewed life through this sacred lens, others would see what Christ has done for them everywhere they go by simply seeing married couples all around. If you're married, you're a walking picture of the Gospel. The real question is, how does your marriage make the Gospel look to others? As a father, it's your responsibility to represent Christ in this picture and this is no easy task.

While a married couple is already a walking display of the Gospel, teaching others about this truth will help them realize it. "For the husband is the head of the wife even as Christ is the head of the church, his body, and is himself its Savior" (Ephesians 5:23). While both parents do share a role in the raising of children, I believe in scripture we see the responsibility of leading the household given to the man. As husband and father, it's your responsibility to not only lead your children but your wife, too. Fathers – this is God's design and it goes back to the beginning.

THE FALL

Genesis chapter three describes "the fall" and in this chapter, it's critically important to see how it all plays out. "Now the serpent was more crafty than any of the wild animals the Lord God had made. He said to the woman, 'Did God really say, You must not eat from any tree in the garden?'" (Genesis 3:1 NIV).

We can see in scripture that Satan doesn't approach Eve with roaring anger towards God. This would have been obvious that he's trying to trick her. No, as the Bible says, he's crafty. He simply poses a question twisting God's instruction to not eat the fruit of the tree of the knowledge of good and evil.

This is how the devil works. Scripture says he's the father of lies (John 8:44). He's here to seek, kill, and destroy and he'll do it in the most non-obvious way he can if he can get away with it. He doesn't typically walk into a room and say, "I'm the devil and I'm here to destroy you." If you'll notice the tone of the passage, Satan almost comes off like he has Eve's best interest at heart. Almost as if she should be thankful he's there to watch out for her. This is how he works. He wants nothing more than to destroy your life, wreck your marriage, and distract you from being the father God designed you to be.

Why would Satan want to tear down marriages and keep fathers from building their households to follow God? It's because his main desire from the very beginning is to seek the glory only which is deserved by God. If he can tear down marriage and fatherhood, he knows this will move people further away from the picture of God's love through Jesus.

Let's move forward and look at how the rest of the chapter

unfolds. "So when the woman saw that the tree was good for food, and that it was a delight to the eyes, and that the tree was to be desired to make one wise, she took of its fruit and ate, and she also gave some to her husband who was with her, and he ate" (Genesis 3:6).

This single moment fractured everything. Adam and Eve both sinned. Now, everything was going to change. Nothing would ever be the same again and the perfect fellowship they experienced with God before this moment was now broken. They realized they were naked, and were ashamed. Sin has entered the world and its destructive path was already in full swing.

You might have read this passage numerous times in your life but have you ever noticed what happens next? Did you see how Eve was the one who ate the forbidden fruit first and gave it to Adam? Have you ever noticed whom God confronts first? Here is where it's critical as a man to understand your responsibility within your household. Eve may have been the one who first ate the fruit, but let's see whom God confronts about the sinful action which just took place. "But the Lord God called to the man and said to him, 'Where are you?'" (Genesis 3:9). See what it says? The Lord God called to *the man*. He didn't call Eve but went looking for Adam.

It was Adam who was responsible for his household. His leadership and oversight had slipped. Now they were suffering the consequences of their actions. Adam knew not to eat the fruit of this tree, as did Eve. I'm not implying the sins your wife commits are your fault, this isn't the case. Eve knew not to eat of the tree, too, and it was her flesh that led to this sinful desire.

We see this in the following verse, "When the woman saw that the fruit of the tree was good for food and pleasing to the eye, and also desirable for gaining wisdom, she took some and ate it..." (Genesis 3:6 NIV).

They both sinned. However, I believe God approached Adam first because it was his responsibility to watch over his household. He let his guard down and now sin entered the world. As men, husbands, and fathers, we have a huge responsibility. God never said it would be easy but it is an incredible opportunity.

Marriage is a commitment because Jesus is committed to us. It wouldn't be right to discuss the joys of marriage without discussing the trials of divorce and its effect on those around us. Divorce was never part of God's plan because as you've seen in the picture of marriage described above, you wouldn't ever separate Christ and his church. If you've grown up in a divorced household or have been through a divorce yourself, I'm sure you can see how this experience wasn't easy for anyone.

If you are a father who is divorced, it's important to be kind to an ex-wife even though it might be difficult. As fathers, we have to set the example we want our children to follow. We can't let sin reign in our life regardless of circumstances. Your children will respect you more and you'll show the love of God through your actions instead of hateful words.

Fathers, it's our job to protect our households at all costs from the devastating effects of not being responsible for our wives, children, and the direction of our families. If we don't change this now, at any moment it could all be gone.

FAST FORWARD

Before we wrap up this chapter, I want you to imagine the end of your life. You're sitting in a hospital bed right now. The lights in the room are all off except for the dim light right above you. It's a little after midnight and all is quiet on your hospital floor. The TV is off and the chairs in the room are left in the spots where your last visitors moved them. You can faintly hear the second-hand tick on the clock on the wall and you're not sure if you'll even make it through the night.

It's at this moment that you start thinking about all you could have done and all you still want to do. You can't go back and change how you will raise your children. You can't go back and show your wife what it's like to sacrificially love her. You can't teach your family how the harmful effects of the culture around them don't reflect God's design. There's no more time to read the Bible to your children or teach them how to pray. All you can do is wait until it's over.

This grim and dark picture isn't a made-up story but a reality for many fathers every day. As you read this book right now, there are fathers in this situation wishing they had done it differently and done it well. Will you be the father who is agonizing over what he didn't do or the father who can rest in life's darkest moment knowing he served his family well? Which one will you be? It's up to you.

In this chapter, we've looked at the role of a father and learned who a father is in relation to their family. We've seen God's design for marriage and the harmful effects of life outside of it. We've seen the ramifications of children who grow up in a fatherless household and the cultural shift in the world around us. We've discussed topics and questions which your children will face. We've reflected on your earthly father and the characteristics he portrayed to you growing up.

We've learned what God's design is for man and his role within the household. We learned work can be an act of worship as God designed us to care for his creation. We discussed how Satan will use any means necessary to destroy your marriage and the lives of your children. Lastly, we envisioned our final moments of life and what we would be thinking about as a father. These are weighty and difficult topics, all of which need a framework in place to guide us along the way. Thankfully, even though we're not perfect fathers, we can however learn from the one who is.

At the end of each chapter, there will be questions to think about over the material we just read. Don't try to quickly answer these questions. Take a moment to pause and be honest with yourself. Each chapter will also include areas to pray over as a father. Use these to help guide your prayers and ask God to grow you closer to him.

QUESTIONS FOR FATHERS

1. What scares you the most about being a father?
2. What did your father do well when you were growing up?
3. What would you regret as a father if you were to die tonight?

PRAYER FOR FATHERS

Pray and ask God to help you reflect him to your family.

2

THE OLD MAN

As a father, you can probably relate to a large amount of whining you hear all too often from your children. I'm writing this with a smile because in my household you're gently asked, "Are you whining?" when your requests sound overly embellished. Typically, our children recognize their tone, admit their wrongdoing, and move on. Whining isn't ever pleasant but it is fairly normal for children. It's not something they outgrow overnight, but as they age it just changes into a different context.

If your children are young, you might hear things like, "I don't want to go to bed," or "I don't want to eat my broccoli." If you have teenagers you've likely heard, "Why can't I stay out late?" or "But all the other kids are doing it." These phrases seem foreign to us as parents but we've all said them ourselves at some point in our own life. While these phrases are unnecessary, you hope over time they'll start to disappear.

As fathers, we don't expect our children to act like mature adults because, well, they're children and children behave as such. Children don't understand why broccoli keeps them healthy and plenty of sleep helps them grow. Teenagers don't think about the ramifications of their decisions so parents have to "disappoint" them to make sure they don't get into trouble.

Another common trait most children share is their love for milk. My kids love to drink milk. They pretty much drink it by the gallon, almost literally. Each morning they start their breakfast with a glass of milk and eat waffles or pancakes made by my wife. Milk provides essential nutrients to help make their bones strong.

Before my kids started drinking milk from a cup, they were drinking milk from a bottle. At the time, this was the only food their little bodies could handle. They weren't mature enough to process the food that we, as adults, take for granted.

As my children have grown, we've introduced foods to them, as one naturally does. They are now ready for more. It would, however, be strange if my children never moved to solid food. While milk was completely suitable for their needs when they were little, it doesn't provide all the necessities they need as adults.

FATHERS ON MILK

Paul speaks to this concept in 1 Corinthians. "I fed you with milk, not solid food, for you were not ready for it. And even now you are not yet ready" (1 Corinthians 3:2). As a father, I want you to think about your spiritual journey up to this point in your life. Think of your relationship with Jesus. Are you still on spiritual milk because you're not ready for solid food? I'm not able to answer this question for you.

As we mentioned earlier, milk is good. We all have been on milk as little children. However, as we matured we moved to solid food because this is what we needed and it's also true for your relationship with Jesus. Have you moved on from milk to solid food? If you haven't, why not? "Jesus Christ is the same yesterday and today and forever" (Hebrews 13:8). He isn't changing and he hasn't gone anywhere. Have you walked away from growing closer to him? Have you put your relationship on pause? If so, are you planning to stay on spiritual milk for the rest of your life?

This book is about fatherhood and the responsibility of being a father. As we mentioned earlier, children taking care of children would be foolish. Could it be that we as fathers are still children because inwardly, we are still on spiritual milk? How can we be ready to raise our children when we're no more mature ourselves?

Are you reading God's word daily? Are you asking God to reveal sinful areas of your life? When was the last time you told someone you would pray for them, and then actually did it? When was the last time you prayed for more than the meal you were eating, if you do at all? Do you read the Bible to your kids? Have you challenged them to start reading it on their own? Do your children know Jesus personally? If not, are you praying for the Holy Spirit to work on their heart and reveal himself to them? If these examples sound foreign to you, there's work to be done.

Before we can spend any time serving our children, we have to work on ourselves. We have to look inwardly and ask God to reveal to us where we currently are in a relationship with him. We can't serve others if we aren't serving Jesus. This is crucial to the fatherhood framework and it's the very first step.

It's easy to point out the faults of others but it's hard to admit the struggles in our own life. Do you know the definition of a hypocrite? "You hypocrite, first take the log out of your own eye, and then you will see clearly to take the speck out of your brother's eye" (Matthew 7:5). The Bible is full of great examples. It's thousands of years old and this picture is just as true today as it was back then. Can you imagine someone walking around with a giant splinter sticking out of their eye while telling others to pull one out of their eye? It's crazy, but we do it every day.

Most fathers won't take their role seriously. They'll let the busyness of life take over, and before you know it, their children will have moved out. True fatherhood is about reflection and change. Change is hard and that's why most people don't do it. Ever had a New Year's resolution? Of course, you have. And then at 12:05 a.m., you didn't. Oh well, there's always next year, right? Next year isn't good enough and tomorrow isn't either. It's today fathers – it has to be now.

I'm writing this chapter with the deepest love I have for you because we need each other in this fatherhood journey. I'm not perfect and neither are you. We all need to continually be formed by the power of God. A community of men who will stop at nothing less than raising God-fearing households without compromise is unstoppable. "What then shall we say to these things? If God is for us, who can be against us?" (Romans 8:31).

Your relationship with Jesus must be the number one priority in your life because everything else hangs in the balance. You won't have a compass for fatherhood if you aren't working on your relationship with your Heavenly Father. You won't know what to do when times get tough, and they will get tough.

The Bible says, "Consider it pure joy, my brothers and sisters, whenever you face trials of many kinds, because you know that the testing of your faith produces perseverance" (James 1:2-3 NIV). Did you notice it doesn't say *if* you face trials? It says *when* you face trials. Trials are coming – it's guaranteed. You might just be getting out of a trial, or unfortunately, you may be headed right into one.

WHOM WOULD JESUS BE?

As a father, the most important relationship in your life has to be Jesus. He should take the number one spot. Jesus needs to be before your wife, children, and everything else. If you get this out of order, everything else will fall apart.

Here's something I want you to think about. If your relationship with Jesus was represented by a real person in your life, how much would you know about him/her? Jesus knows everything about you. This exercise represents how much you know about him. Whom would this person be in your life?

Would Jesus be your wife? Someone whom you know the

intimate details of their life. Someone you share everything with, and who knows almost all there is to know about you.

Would Jesus be like a coworker? Someone whom you spend some time with throughout the week but never get too personal with. You make fairly basic small talk but at 5 o'clock, you're gone.

Or would Jesus be like the barista of your local coffee shop, who you feel like you've seen before but don't remember his name or anything about his life other than you run into him once in a while? Which person would he be?

This is a powerful exercise and it goes to show if we're actively building a relationship with him or if we've stalled out years ago. When was the last time you pulled out your Bible to hear from God? I mean a real Bible and not your phone. If you're trying to remember where you even keep your Bible you probably need to turn up the heat. Don't know where to start reading? That's ok, it works like all other books. Open the cover and start on the first page. You'll read left to right and top to bottom turning each page as you finish.

I've seen several reading plans over the years which all have similar taglines like, "Spend five minutes with God," or other short daily devotionals. Who invented these programs? Is this what it's come to? Fathers, are we so incapable of developing a meaningful relationship with our creator that they have to market books based on the shortest amount of time? It's almost like the authors sat around and said, "We want these people to have a meaningful relationship with the Lord but it takes time and dedication. Since we know it's unlikely they'll do it, we'll just try to get them to read for five minutes daily and call it good."

We wouldn't apply this logic to anything else in our life. This would be like only driving our car to the end of the street or eating three bites of a sandwich and throwing the rest in the trash. Do you go to the gym and only work out for five minutes then leave? Of course not. It's crazy.

Here's the math, if you only spent five minutes with God every day from the time you were 18 years old until the age of 78 (which is the current average lifespan of a male living in the United States), you would have spent a total of 76 days developing your relationship with him.

This isn't even three months and this is assuming you never missed a single day. Not exactly something to write home about. This would be equivalent to the coffee shop barista at best. You would barely know him. Is this the relationship you want to have with God? Is this the foundation you want to have to hold up your house?

As we press on throughout this book, we're going to look at characteristics in which God displays the perfect picture of fatherhood to us and invites us to display this picture to our children. If we are ever going to have a chance of pointing our kids to Jesus, we first must go to work on ourselves.

This will be the hardest chapter in the book because it's directly dealing with our shortcomings. It's always easier to discuss the faults and failures of others while passing over the sins and destructive habits we have either picked up or never put down.

Take time to pray and ask God to start working on your

heart. Maybe it's been a while since you prayed. If so, the Lord welcomes you back with open arms. He's not mad and loves you just as much today as ever. Ask him to reveal to you the sin in your life that you may be holding onto. We all know areas in our life that are personal struggles. These could be lust, anger, covetousness, or even abusive habits. They might be addictions like pornography or alcohol. The list goes on and on. Ask the Holy Spirit to stir you and make these areas evident.

What must you give up to be the father that God designed you to be? Where do you personally struggle? What would you tell your kids not to do, but that you do yourself when they're not around? What would others say is an area of your life that needs work? These are tough questions and should cause a fair amount of wrestling.

Being a follower of Jesus isn't easy. This is a huge misconception. Many people think when they become a follower of Jesus, life magically becomes perfect and they won't struggle with the same issues that they had before. This is incorrect. The struggles of your past will continue to try and draw you back into them. You'll have to wrestle with temptation your entire life.

This chapter is called *The Old Man* and if you're a believer, it's a representation of your past, not your present. Sometimes, that's a phrase people use to represent their father but that's not the meaning of this chapter. The old man that I'm referring to is who you were before Jesus.

Paul talks about this idea of the old man. "Therefore, if anyone is in Christ, he is a new creation. The old has passed away; behold, the new has come" (2 Corinthians 5:17). There has to be a time in your life when you say enough is enough. When are you going to wake up and say, "I'm not going to be a slave to my past sins anymore"? Jesus has set you free from sin through his death, burial, and resurrection, and you will not be the old man anymore.

You were dead in your sins and trespasses, and destined for an eternity without him. God in his goodness reached out to you to pull you from darkness to light. From death to life. From the old man to the new one. The Bible says you are a new creation if you are in Jesus. The old has passed away. Fathers, this is incredible news.

THE WORST SOUND AT NIGHT

My wife and I have a labradoodle named Jack. We got Jack as a puppy two years after we had been married. I was looking to get a dog at the time and wanted a lab but felt the labradoodle was a more modern, upscale version portraying a sophisticated, middle-class working family living in the Midwest. I'm joking, of course, it came down to cute pictures online and I was sold.

He's a ton of fun and great with our kids. At the time of writing this book, Jack is eight years old. The only thing I would change after all of our years together is the fact that Jack eats everything. I mean everything. Quite a few of which are not food.

I can't begin to tell you the number of socks and small children's toys our dog has ingested over the years. It's not uncommon to be playing baseball with my son Titus in the backyard only to see remnants of action figures which have passed completely through the digestive tract of this 85-pound animal.

Jack's file at the veterinarian's office resembles a phone book. If you're reading this right now and wondering what a phone book is, it was an obnoxiously large book in which everyone in your city's name, address, and phone number were published years ago. It was left on your doorstep and every house had one. You could look up the information of anyone you wanted. This was before privacy laws and common sense went mainstream (again, joking).

There is no feeling like being sound asleep in the middle of the night and waking up to the wretched sound of a large animal getting ready to throw up all over your bedroom floor. If you've experienced this in your own house, we are now closer to each other because of it. We are pretty much bonded for life. It's just too bad it's around this moment.

Before my eyes can even remotely see in the dark room, I've abruptly thrown off the sheets and am heading towards the sound, hoping I push Jack onto the hardwood floors in the hallway making what's about to happen easier to clean up. We have since added hardwoods to our bedroom and the dog hasn't been sick since. Go figure.

What makes this entire experience all the more disgusting is after the deed has occurred, you can often find your dog enjoying the meal a second time. For those who have never owned a dog, they do, at times, eat their vomit. Gross. While this is high on the list of completely disgusting animal traits, it's a great representation of how we look when we continue in sin.

Let's look at the following passage of scripture which

reflects what it looks like to stay the old man. "As a dog returns to its vomit, so fools repeat their folly" (Proverbs 26:11 NIV). This is disgusting but you couldn't have a clearer picture from the Bible. Here is what makes this even crazier. The dog in the passage doesn't even realize what he's doing!

The dog thinks he's doing something enjoyable but everyone watching him sees the actual reality. Everyone sees the filth and nastiness which is occurring all while he can't see any of it. This is a picture of sin, yes, our sin. You, me, and everyone in the world who goes back to their sin and doesn't even notice it. This is why we must continually seek God and ask for his help in overcoming our sinful desires. We cannot stay the old man because we've died to the old man.

In scripture, David says, "Search me, O God, and know my heart! Try me and know my thoughts" (Psalm 139:23). David is a man who is interested in changing his ways in this passage. He knows his heart can be a place where sinful desires stay hidden. "The heart is deceitful above all things, and desperately wicked: who can know it?" (Jeremiah 17:9 KJV). Don't trust your heart, trust God.

WHAT IS THIS PLACE?

Every day we can turn on the news to see death and destruction all around us. Murder, rape, theft, greed, fraud, and evil acts so vile it's not even fair to give them words on these pages. Abusive actions happening to children, wars based on pride, and false religions. Disease wreaking havoc on people we love. All of these terrible things have a single source – sin. In essence, what is sin? Sin is anything that goes against God's direction, design, and command. It's everything that is against his very nature.

We read how when Adam and Eve were in the garden, they were in perfect fellowship with God. They had everything they needed. They were naked and not ashamed. Once Satan tempted them and they gave in to this temptation, everything changed. The world became fractured. Everything broken in our world can be traced back to this very moment in time. From this point on, death entered the picture. Death is a part of life. There is not one person who will escape it.

While we can't escape physical death, we can pursue a life where the old man isn't a part of us anymore. Fathers, we can't continue in our sins. We must put off our old ways. We will never be perfect on this side of eternity but we can work daily to put off our old ways. "What shall we say then? Are we to continue in sin that grace may abound? By no means! How can we who died to sin still live in it?" (Romans 6:1-2).

While physical death is inevitable, spiritual death is not. Do you have a relationship with Jesus? If you have been wrestling with your faith for years, or if all of this is just starting to make sense, soon we're going to read a chapter in this book called *Knowing the Father*. In this chapter, we'll discuss who God is and what he has done for us. We'll discuss how you can know him personally.

DISTRACTIONS

Do you ever get distracted? Do you find yourself not present when around your family, at times? Do your wife or children get a back seat to your work or other activities in your life? Got a side hustle that is crushing you? When was the last time you were distracted? What about the last time you were doing something for so long that you simply lost track of time?

Distractions can be extremely subtle because you typically don't wake up to a full-blown addiction in any one area of your life. You probably started down a path that over time led to a habit. Unfortunately, this might have led to an unhealthy one or even a number of them. All fathers are different and how we spend our time looks different to each one of us. Did you notice I didn't say how we spend our *free* time? No, we spend *valuable* time on distractions too, not just our free time.

The issue with distractions is they are a slow-growing problem. Generally, we get used to their feelings and over time we don't even seem to notice them. What are some distractions in your life? What is taking time away from your kids? Most people might think of work, but I think there are several more alternatives. Don't rush this self-reflection because the most precious resource we have in life is time. No matter how much money we make, we'll never get time back. Once it's gone, it's gone.

Perhaps you think your work or side hustle is all for the right reasons. It's just one more email or one more phone call. You tell yourself you'll go to the next baseball game or dance recital but this meeting is too important to miss. Maybe you think the money you're making is to better the life of your family, but if it's costing you time with them, I'm sure they would rather have a present father than a wealthy dad that they don't see.

The Bible says, "For what will it profit a man if he gains the whole world and forfeits his soul? Or what shall a man give in return for his soul?" (Matthew 16:26). This verse is speaking about people who get caught up in life and miss salvation through Jesus. However, I think it can also be a great reminder of what is important in life. What will it profit you to make a million dollars? What will it change in your life? Your family will be the same and you'll still have the same problems you struggle with today, likely more.

Maybe you're the dad who spends his weekends hunting or at the golf course. Do you watch every football game on Sundays while your kids play alone? Would Netflix consider you a truly valued customer? Perhaps you spend too much time online or with your phone. There are many distractions and this isn't an exhaustive list. You might even be the dad who brings their work into every moment of life.

I'm not going to tell you I'm perfect and don't get distracted. However, I will say I've taken some rather drastic measures in my own life over the last few years to prioritize what's important to me. I've put up certain barriers to not put myself into distracting situations rather than hoping I can be disciplined enough to manage them. Not allowing temptation is much easier than trying to resist it. I'm asking you to evaluate how you spend your time and list out what areas in your life need adjustments.

I'm not going to ask you to burn your TV or phone in some self-deprecating ritual, I'm going to ask you to begin thinking about behavior modifications and barriers you can work on to prevent distractions in your life. I don't want to give the impression I'm perfect in this area so I'll give you some examples from my own life. I'm not any better than you but I'm trying to work each day to be more present with the time I'm given by God.

In 2020, I came to the realization I was spending too much time on my phone. It wasn't costing me time with my family or straining any relationships, I just personally realized while it wasn't wrong, it was a waste of my time. I decided to delete several of my online accounts completely.

This wasn't just a break from them but it was a full-fledged breakup. I permanently deleted these accounts and my years of history, pictures, and connections were all gone in an instant. I no longer needed to see what my friends had for breakfast or where they went on vacation. I'd rather enjoy a meal together and talk about what's new in their life than see it online anyway. My phone today more closely resembles a phone I had in high school than the latest app-filled device it was designed to be. I still use a few apps but have since removed the rest. I also set almost all my notifications to off.

Some of you might be thinking, "There's no way I could turn off notifications for work emails." Well, if this is truly the case, you might need to find a different job. I work hard but I have a computer at my desk which shows me all of my emails. If there is an emergency when I'm out of the office, my colleagues know to call me. Otherwise, when I'm not at work, I can check email when it's convenient.

My phone typically stays in my bag at the office unless I need to make a call or send a message, and I leave it in my bag when I get home until my kids go to bed. I use the web functionality minimally and would rather grab my computer to go online, anyway. This helps me consider if what I'm about to do is that important.

I don't reach for my phone first thing when I wake up and I only take it off the charger when I walk out the door to head to the office. The few things I do enjoy on it are streaming music, listening to audiobooks, making phone calls, and some text messaging to catch up with people in my life. Otherwise, it's not a big necessity for me.

I've even started leaving it behind at times when I run errands or take a walk. My goal for my daily screen time is under one hour and I'm pretty close. This all may sound wild to you but don't knock it till you try it. It's no different from someone who doesn't keep cookies in their house because they know they'll eat them all. The best offense is a good defense. Want to know the best way to not overeat cookies? Don't buy cookies. I've just applied the same idea to my phone.

A distracted father is an absent father, even if it's just for a few moments because all of those moments add up to lost time that you'll never get back. Be proactive dads and get rid of distractions. It may be a phone, hobby, or vocation but they all are detrimental to ourselves and our children if not properly managed. If you are struggling to think about what these might be in your life, ask your family, they'll know.

In the Bible, Paul says, "When I was a child, I spoke like a child, I thought like a child, I reasoned like a child. When I became a man, I gave up childish ways" (1 Corinthians 13:11). Are you ready to put away childish things in your life? Only you can decide.

DEATH TO LIFE

I love baptism Sunday at church. Baptism is one of the most beautiful representations of the Gospel we have. If you are a believer and have given your life to Jesus, you've likely been baptized. Baptism is the first act of obedience once someone becomes a believer.

Baptism is a picture of the life, death, burial, and resurrection of Jesus. When someone steps into the baptism water they are professing to the world that they have repented of their sins and asked Jesus to be their Lord and savior. Standing in the water is the final representation of the *old man*. Do you remember when you were baptized?

Remember, the old man went down into the water but he didn't come back out of it. The new man came out of it and his life should look different. The picture of Jesus putting to death all sin for all mankind and raising us to life anew is nothing short of incredible. It's true life that you can only find in him.

If it's been a while since you were baptized, remember this picture and what it represented in your life. You were standing there telling the world what Jesus had done for you. You were showing everyone else what it looks like to go from death to life. "Therefore we are buried with him by baptism into death: that like as Christ was raised up from the dead by the glory of the Father, even so we also should walk in newness of life" (Romans 6:4 KJV).

If you're a follower of Jesus but haven't taken the step of obedience in baptism, I want to encourage you to take this next step in faith. Like the picture of marriage we spoke about earlier, I believe baptism is as much for those watching, as it is for the individual. The public display of baptism allows others to see a picture of the Gospel. This allows others to think about whom you have decided to trust and follow. It allows them to see the life change Jesus makes when he comes and brings someone from death to life.

THE PHARISEES

I don't think there was a more frustrating group of people in the New Testament to Jesus than the Pharisees. They were a group who constantly accused Jesus of doing wrong when they believed it went against their Jewish teachings and their traditions. They were missing the bigger picture and everything that Jesus was doing during his ministry. The Pharisees were not trying to *do* right, they were simply trying to *look* right. As fathers, we're not trying to raise moral children; we're trying to raise children who reflect Jesus. Scripture doesn't speak highly of the Pharisees. It speaks quite poorly of them.

At the beginning of the New Testament in the book of Matthew, John the Baptist comes ushering in a new era of repentance. He's down at the Jordan River baptizing people before Jesus begins his ministry. When he sees the Pharisees coming towards him, he says the following, "But when he saw many of the Pharisees and Sadducees coming to his baptism, he said to them, 'You brood of vipers! Who warned you to flee from the wrath to come?'" (Matthew 3:7). This is strong language. John isn't messing around. He knows their hearts are hard and they are set in their ways. Fathers, don't be like the Pharisees, and don't raise Pharisees.

Further in Matthew, Jesus speaks to them about their appearance to others, "'Woe to you, teachers of the law and Pharisees, you hypocrites! You are like whitewashed tombs, which look beautiful on the outside but on the inside are full of the bones of the dead and everything unclean. In the same way, on the outside you appear to people as righteous but on the inside you are full of hypocrisy and wickedness'" (Matthew 23:27-28 NIV). Jesus called them whitewashed tombs. They appear nice to everyone on the outside but inside they are dead.

Throughout the New Testament, this tension exists between the Pharisees and Jesus. They are stubborn, self-righteous, and unforgiving, and think of themselves above others. Do any of these traits seem like you? Could you be a modern-day Pharisee?

YOU'RE THE DOOR

Do you check to make sure your front door is locked before you go to bed? I bet you do. Why is it you check to see if the door is locked? You check because you want to keep bad things from coming inside your home. You want to keep potential thieves from entering and destroying all that you have worked for. What if I told you that your front door wasn't the way things get inside your home? No fathers, the actual front door to your home, is you.

You are the guardian of what comes into your home. As a

father, you are responsible for protecting your family from the harmful things in the world. I'm not speaking in terms of a thief attempting to break into your home in the middle of the night. No, we have locks and security systems for those kinds of things. I'm speaking about what you just let walk right into your house.

What kind of shows are your kids streaming? Do you even know what they watch? What are they texting their friends about? What are your kids looking at on the computer? What friends are you allowing them to have over and influence their life? You can't control what happens in the outside world. No one can. However, you can protect your household, but are you?

What would you do if Satan rang your doorbell and said, "I happened to be in the neighborhood and wanted to know if I could come inside for a bit?" Without question, you would slam the door in his face, but are you letting him inside in other ways? Satan would love nothing more than for you to simply not think these things are a big deal. It makes his job quite a bit easier when you're both working together, even though you don't realize it.

The Bible says, "Be sober-minded; be watchful. Your adversary the devil prowls around like a roaring lion, seeking someone to devour" (1 Peter 5:8). He might be walking around your neighborhood, but you don't have to let him walk into your home. It's up to you.

THIS IS WAR

Fathers, you're at war. Did you know it? You might think of war as two countries battling each other over land or political power. You're in a war every day whether you know it or not. This fight isn't with the physical world, although at times I know it can feel this way. No, you're part of a much bigger war with eternal consequences.

Satan and his army are spending their time trying to wreak havoc on the world and destroy any appearance of a loving God. "For we do not wrestle against flesh and blood, but against the rulers, against the authorities, against the cosmic powers over this present darkness, against the spiritual forces of evil in the heavenly places" (Ephesians 6:12).

It's always easier to prepare for a battle before you're in one, rather than learning to fight in the midst of it. Are you watching for the ways that Satan is waging war against you and your family? Are you putting on the armor of God to protect yourself from his ways? You won't see missiles or gunfire from this war. You'll see cracks form in various places before everything breaks down. Be on guard fathers.

LOOK BACK BUT MOVE FORWARD

In this chapter, we've examined ourselves and the sins which pull us away from God. We've identified several areas we can explore and ask God to start changing our hearts. We've talked about several things in the chapter which can make us feel inadequate and a failure in this fatherhood game.

The idea is to not make you feel like you're failing as a father, but instead help you identify areas you need to change. It's ok to look at the past even if the past is messy. It's just not ok to stay this way. You can look back but you have to move forward. Don't let the past write your future. Today is a blessing from God. You're alive and it's not too late to start being the father God wants you to be.

To start becoming a better father, you need to realize one very important thing. If you're a follower of Jesus, you're a son in God's family. You've been adopted into his family through Jesus and his sacrifice on the cross. You no longer are a stranger outside his provision but are welcomed right inside to sit with him.

In the first two chapters, we looked at who a father is, and how we are a new creation once we give our life to Jesus. The old man is dead and the new man is alive in Christ. This reality opens up a direct connection to God through Jesus and he goes before us in our requests. In the following chapters, we're going to look at how God has modeled to us the ultimate picture of fatherhood.

Before we leave this chapter and begin to look at the characteristics of fatherhood God demonstrates to each of us, I thought it would be helpful to see a passage of scripture that represents how a follower of Jesus should strive to be. I can't think of another passage that displays this more clearly than the following. "Blessed is the man who walks not in the counsel of the wicked, nor stands in the way of sinners, nor sits in the seat of scoffers; but his delight is in the law of the Lord, and on his law he meditates day and night. He is like a tree planted by streams of water that yields its fruit in its season, and its leaf does not wither. In all that he does, he prospers" (Psalm 1:1-3).

The man described above is the type of father you want to be. This man delights in the law of the Lord. He's in the word daily, he's praying for his heart to change, he's watching out for his household, he's serving his kids, and he's loving his wife. It says he's like a tree planted by streams of water. I love this imagery. The tree gets the water it needs to survive and produce fruit because it stays close to its source of life. When we stay close to God, we'll thrive too.

It goes on to say in all that he does, he prospers. It doesn't mean that there won't be hard days. There will be good days, bad days, birthdays, sick days, death days, and everything in between. It doesn't mean we will be rich or have everything we want in life. There isn't a promise of health or security, but this man prospers because he has everything he needs to get through it all. When you trust the perfect father, you'll prosper too.

QUESTIONS FOR FATHERS

1. As a believer, are you still on spiritual milk?
2. What person in your life would represent your relationship with Jesus?
3. What distractions in your life do you need to change?

PRAYER FOR FATHERS

Pray and ask God to reveal where you might be letting Satan have a foothold in your home.

3

A FATHER LOVES

I remember going to college with the fresh anticipation any young adult has when they're off on this grand adventure. I had the freedom I'd never experienced before and was in a place surrounded by people from all over the world. While I was attending an in-state school, I looked forward to calling Missouri State University my campus for the next four years. I was excited about my future and all the possibilities it might entail. My entire life was ahead of me and I was ready to tackle it. I wasn't sure what I would be doing but each day seemed like exploring the world in an entirely new light.

The very first class I had in college was English 110. I find it funny that most of us have taken English since elementary school, but somehow in college we need to pay to revisit fundamentals once again. Regardless, I was willing to take any class they offered as long as *she* was in it.

The *she* I am referring to was, well, at the time an unknown girl I'd never met. We were given the assignment to write about a trip that had a profound impact on our life. The class dismissed and sadly, she did too. Thankfully another English class was right around the corner and I was hoping she would be right back in the same spot.

The next week, there she was. She sat two seats away from me making it hard to strike up a conversation. Unfortunately, another woman was keeping us apart. Not another woman in my life, just literally another woman in between us (this seems like a good dad joke).

We were asked to randomly pass our papers around to each other for a peer review. I think if someone had been watching me I must have looked ridiculous. As her paper traded with the girl between us and then made its way to me, I wasn't about to hand it off to the next person. No, this was my peer review. I held on to it with the grip of 1,000 men. This was my woman. Well, not yet anyway.

When the shuffling finally stopped, everyone started reviewing the paper they had in front of them. Thankfully I had hers. She wrote about a mission trip she took earlier in life. I had just returned from a mission trip myself in the summer. Now I'm not going to attempt to over-spiritualize the following (well, maybe a little bit) but suffice it to say, it was good.

Obviously, I interpreted this as a sign from God for me to approach her directly after class, immediately ask for her hand in marriage, have two children, and live happily ever after. I mean, what are the odds two different people have taken mission trips and ended up at the same public university? I guess they are pretty high but I was still excited.

What happened next goes as one would expect. She kept continuing to pester me after class due to my good looks and impressive physique about taking her out on a date. I finally relented. Later on, after much determination, she begged me to marry her and whisk her off into her dream romance. This is how I tell the story to new people we meet, but their look usually displays a sense of suspicion. You're probably not buying this version of this story either. Let's get back on track.

Ok, so there I was reading about this beautiful girl in my English class who went on a mission trip. This was almost too easy. I had this moment when I felt like Adam back in the garden, who after seeing God create a woman, he looks up at the sky to God and says, "Thank you!" I did, however, get the courage to ask her out after class and even though she didn't know me, she said yes.

A small tangent before moving forward. I'm always intrigued by the idea of online dating. This wasn't a thing when I was growing up as it hadn't gone mainstream because smartphones had just started to take off. When I was growing up, I had to muster up the guts to go talk to the unknown girl and be willing to face the likely outcome of rejection.

I felt like a prehistoric man having to go face a grizzly bear with a stick I fashioned a small pointy rock to at the tip. Nowadays, online dating feels like the equivalent of going to the grocery store and standing around pondering the options before you make a decision. I'm not speaking negatively about this opportunity that didn't exist for me. If you've found your wife using online dating, that's fantastic. I'm simply fascinated with the process as we've figured out a way to skirt the idea of rejection. As they say, to be a kid these days.

The short story, at this point, is to tell you we dated for the next few years and then got married the year after we graduated. I remember standing in the church holding hands and staring at each other. This moment was, again, a picture of Christ and the church and I was blessed with the opportunity to display it to everyone in the room that day. While this book is about fatherhood, needless to say, I wouldn't be a father without Amy. Our first child was a son named Titus and God gifted us with him six years into our marriage.

WHAT IS LOVE?

The first characteristic of fatherhood we're going to discuss is love. What is love? How would you describe love to someone else? Who in your life do you love? How do you even display love? We all use the term correctly and incorrectly. "I love my wife" is a correct use of the word. But saying, "I love this cake" would be an incorrect usage. No, you don't love the cake like you love your wife. You like the cake, perhaps, but you don't love it. Since love should be more reserved in our vocabulary, what does it mean?

In the Bible, it says, "Anyone who does not love does not know God, because God is love" (1 John 4:8). God's love is the basis for everything in existence. It's the foundation for the creation of the world and everything in it. God didn't need to create us to be happy or to fill some hole in his life. He was perfectly content with the other two persons of the Trinity. God has always existed as Father, Son, and Holy Spirit and he was fully satisfied.

Love is God's very nature; it's who he is. He has our best interests at heart and it is out of his love for us that he created us. You might be wondering what Godly love looks like and how you might display it to your family. We have a great description of love and how God displays love to us in 1 Corinthians. We often hear this passage at weddings but it's the perfect description of how our Heavenly Father displays love and wants us to as fathers. It says, "Love is patient, love is kind. It does not envy, it does not boast, it is not proud. It does not dishonor others, it is not self-seeking, it is not easily angered, it keeps no record of wrongs. Love does not delight in evil but rejoices with the truth. It always protects, always trusts, always hopes, always perseveres. Love never fails" (1 Corinthians 13:4-8 NIV).

What would you say if I asked how your life looks as a father compared to these characteristics above? Are you a patient father, or do you get frustrated easily? Are you kind to your children and those around you, or is your speech laced with hurtful words? Do you spend your time discontent with what you have and focus on what you don't have? Are you prideful and the first person to direct attention to yourself? Do you speak well of others or would your family know the people who have wronged you? What about anger? Are your children afraid of you? What about the people you work with? Do you present a calm loving attitude daily or are you always just a moment away from an outburst?

We tend to forget our family is not the only group of people with whom we can display God's picture of fatherhood. We display fatherhood to everyone we meet. If you didn't already know, as a believer, you live in a glass house. People are watching you and seeing how you react to the various situations of life. You will either lead people toward Jesus or away from him, but no one will stay the same. How you act to others in public is a reflection of how you act at home. If you can't handle seemingly insignificant moments in life, you'll be unable to handle the truly difficult trials which come your way.

What do you say when you get cut off in traffic or end up with the wrong meal in a drive-through? Do you lose your mind or simply brush it off? Your children are watching everything you do and they are learning how to treat others in the process. When your kids do or say something wrong, have you ever asked, "Where did you learn that?" Be prepared for the answer you might hear.

While I'm not asking you to be passive in character, I'm asking you to look at Jesus. Use everyday situations like these to teach your children to handle them with love. Instead of shouting at the car that cut you off, could you use the moment to explain to your children how it's always best to keep focused when driving because others may not always be paying attention? Could you open your takeout at home to find something wrong and just eat it anyway.

These small behaviors begin to add up and they'll make a big difference to those around you. If you do this enough, your children will start to not only think their father is a good father but more importantly, they'll want to understand *why*.

Why is it that dad doesn't lose his mind in traffic? Why is it that dad walks in the door smiling after a hard day at work? Why is it that dad is choosing to miss his annual hunting trip because his kid's team made the playoffs? Why does dad read his Bible every morning before doing anything else? Why did dad run up to the church three times this week to help out?

It's love, and as we'll see shortly, love is a sacrifice. You know your actions are not because you've done anything right. You're doing it out of love for your Heavenly Father so your children see Jesus.

THE BRIDGE

The second that your actions cause your children to wonder *why* you're behaving a certain way is a crucial moment in time. This is what I call the *bridge* in the fatherhood framework. The bridge is the moments in your life where your actions as a father will either connect them to Jesus or steer them away from him. We build bridges and tear them down every day. Most of the time without knowing it. Jesus is the only one who could have built the bridge for us to get to God, but as fathers, we can build the bridge for others to get to Jesus.

Your children won't have to wonder why you're a good father because they'll know you're trying to display the love of Jesus. You're simply reflecting on what a good father does because you're keeping your eyes fixed on your Heavenly Father. Your actions should reflect his goodness in your life so your spouse, children, and everyone around you will see him. As fathers, we're not trying to raise moral children. We're trying to raise children who desire to serve Jesus. If they learn to love him, they'll desire to do what's right in his eyes.

LOVE GOD. LOVE OTHERS.

God's love is shown throughout the entire Bible. However, the Bible isn't a book about you, it's a book about God. When Jesus is asked, what is the greatest commandment, he responds with "...'Love the Lord your God with all your heart and with all your soul and with all your mind.' This is the first and greatest commandment. And the second is like it: 'Love your neighbor as yourself.' All the Law and the Prophets hang on these two commandments" (Matthew 22:36-40 NIV).

First Jesus says to love the Lord your God with all your heart, soul, and mind. As we look back on chapter two of this book, we're reminded that as fathers we must first seek after God. We cannot truly love others if we're not loving God first. We must love God above our spouse, children, and everything else. Your relationship with God must come first in your life because it's only through this relationship that you will understand how to love and serve your children.

The word *all* is written three times in this passage because you can't be partially committed to God. You have to be all in or all out. There is no middle ground. You can't only love God in the good times. You can't only love God if you get the job you want. You can't only love God if he heals your illness. God is asking for all of you because he gave all of him. He sacrificed himself on the cross in totality. There was nothing he held back. He did it first and he did it out of love.

In the second part of this passage, Jesus goes on to say love your neighbor as yourself. This means everyone. It's your family, your actual neighbors, coworkers, strangers at the store, the car that cut you off, and the fast food worker who messed up your order. It is the people who look like you and the people who don't. It's those who serve God and those who don't. God doesn't show partiality and neither should you. There is no bridge like love. Don't you want your children to remember you as a father who loved others? I sure do.

I want to take a moment to address a very serious distinction when it comes to love. There is a massive misconception taking place in our culture today. It's the idea that love equals acceptance. This is wrong. You are not loving by allowing or accepting things in life that go against scripture. This is true in your own life and the lives of others. God is the authority, not you. His word is the standard, not yours. You don't get to decide what's right, he does. The Bible isn't a buffet where you can come take the things you like and leave the rest. His word is Holy from cover to cover, not just the parts you want to hear. You can take it all or you can leave it all but there's no third option. You can love people but you can't love sin. You can love your neighbor but you can't support their sin. You can love your friends but you can't love their sins. You can't love God and love sin.

There must be a separation between loving your neighbor as someone created in the image of God and not loving sin. To love and accept anything contrary to what God has established is unloving. It breaks down the picture of who God is and tears down the bridge which leads others to Jesus. Don't miss what

I'm saying, you can love your neighbor, but you can't accept and love sin. "Do not love the world or the things in the world. If anyone loves the world, the love of the Father is not in him" (1 John 2:15).

As soon as we start deciding what is right, we make a statement that we no longer need God. We are saying we know what is best for us and we bring ourselves right back into the garden. We are back in the same place Adam and Eve were and now we are the ones holding the fruit and thinking it looks good. How did that work out for them?

LOVE IS A SACRIFICE

You can't have love without sacrifice. Love is a sacrifice because it signifies you're putting others before yourself. Sacrifice is hard and it should be. Know the opposite of love? Selfishness. Love and selfishness are antonyms. They are incompatible with one another. As fathers, we need to model selflessness, not selfishness. Fathers sacrifice many things for their families. I know many of you reading this book work hard to provide for your household, but sacrifice goes beyond paying the bills. True sacrifice is hard because you must die to yourself in the process. You have to put the desires of others in front of your own. Do you know who put others before himself? Jesus.

Probably the most famous verse in the Bible is John 3:16. We see this verse plastered on everything from billboards to sweatshirts. It's on coffee mugs and signs we hang in our homes. No matter how many times you've seen this verse, don't miss the meaning. This single verse is the best picture any of us will ever have of love. Most of us know it by heart. You know how it starts, "For God so loved." What is it that he loved? It says, "the world." This is everyone. You, me, and all our neighbors. The following part is where sacrifice enters the picture, the next part of the verse says, "that he gave." Sacrifice requires giving, it requires giving of yourself. Are you a giving father? If you're a believer, your father is a giver. He's the ultimate giver.

Let's continue. What did he give? He gave "his one and only son." He gave everything. He left nothing and he did it all because he loves you. Jesus' death on the cross displays God as the ultimate giver. He's paid the ultimate sacrifice. He did all of this because he didn't want you to spend an eternity separated from him. He did what you couldn't do. He laid down his life so that you could have life. Why did he do all of this? Love.

LOVE NEVER FAILS

If you knew you were going to be killed tomorrow, how would you spend your last night? In scripture, Jesus knew he was going to be killed. Would you go see a sports game or take a quick trip with friends? Would you spend all the money you had on stuff you've always wanted? Perhaps you would throw a huge party with the best food you could find.

For thousands of years, the world had been waiting on a Messiah to come. Most people expected someone who would be a true warrior in the traditional sense. Someone who would be a battle-scarred victor who would blaze into the world and destroy evil right in its tracks.

Instead, Jesus came into this world born of a virgin and

spent his life serving those around him. This may be a different picture than some were anticipating but he's exactly the savior we all needed. He came into the world at the perfect time to crush sin on a cross. While he died, he didn't stay dead. He was raised to life three days later by God to once and for all break the chains of sin over the world. If you're still wondering what you would do with your last night before death, you might look at how Jesus spent his.

HERE TO SERVE

One of the most humbling stories in the New Testament comes in John chapter 13. In just a few hours Jesus would be nailed to a cross to suffer the most painful death the Romans could imagine. If you haven't read much about the process of crucifixion, it's basically the worst possible way you can think of to die. It's a slow and agonizing process where they nailed your hands and feet to a wooden cross while you were completely alive. To breathe, you would have to pull yourself up using your arms and legs since you were in a suspended position. Over time, the weight of your body would make you weaker, making it harder and harder to get each breath. Eventually, you would be unable to pull yourself up to take a breath and would suffocate.

Sometimes, the individuals who were crucified stayed alive longer than expected. In this case, the soldiers would break their legs to speed up the dying process. If you can't use your legs, you'll be unable to push yourself up for air. All of this was done in a public setting so others would fear Rome and the possibility that this could happen to them.

Jesus knew in a few hours that this was going to be him. He could have run away, called angels to rescue him, or decided to do something for himself. So what did he do? He spent his time doing what he has been doing since the beginning of creation. He decided to spend his final night loving his people.

Jesus spent his last few hours washing the feet of his disciples. Why would he do this? He did this because it symbolized him coming to wash away the sins of the world. He came to serve those who couldn't help themselves. He came to clean up the mess we made so we could know him. Jesus won't leave you in your darkest hour, because he spent his darkest hour loving you.

LOVE LIKE JESUS

In this chapter, we've seen how God is love and how he demonstrated the ultimate picture of love to us on the cross. As a father, look to Jesus and the sacrifice he made as you look to serve your family. Ask yourself, "Where am I not showing love?" As a father, it doesn't matter how old your children get, they'll always be your kids. If they are little, how can you love them well at their current stage of life? If they are grown, how can you continue to love them as adults?

If we model the love of Jesus, there will be nothing but a bridge to the cross. Love never fails. Take time to reflect on where you might need to work on loving your kids. Ask God to reveal to you where love is lacking in your life. Thank God for his love and for those who have loved you. Be a loving father, and reflect the love of the father who first loved you.

QUESTIONS FOR FATHERS

1. Did you show love to your family this week with your time?
2. What are your actions telling your family about love?
3. How did you teach your children about God's love this week?

PRAYER FOR FATHERS

Pray and ask God to help you show love to those around you.

4

A FATHER PROVIDES

When my wife Amy and I got married, we were both employed with our first jobs, and at the time, we didn't have any children. Thankfully, we were able to tithe, pay our bills, save, and purchase some occasional "wants" along the way. This situation might sound familiar to you or it might be very different. Quite often money is tight when you first get married as you're usually just starting out. Where did the provisions of our household come from? Where do they come from in your house?

Was our situation based on our hard work? Was each month just luck? What about yours? How do you think your bills get paid? Take a moment to think about your current situation. While I believe God gives us a sound mind to make wise decisions, there is no denying the fact that God is our provider.

When we had our first child, I suddenly found myself thinking, "Why is baby formula so expensive?" This was the closest I've ever felt to a drug dealer in my life. I would find myself having to go out late at night for a small tin of this very expensive powder. When I returned home, I would attempt to collect the fine dust particles evaporating with each spoonful so as not to waste anything.

MANAGING WELL

As a father, it's your job to manage what God has given you well. Do you have a budget? Do you stick to it? While this book isn't about finances, it's best to understand the first thing about money which is that God provides everything. Everything is the Lord's and you're just borrowing it. The Bible says, "For every beast of the forest is mine, the cattle on a thousand hills" (Psalm 50:10).

When Amy became pregnant with Titus, we decided she would stop teaching and stay home with him. At first, the idea of this was uncomfortable for me. I came from a family where both parents worked and the idea of having both incomes was, in some ways, a false sense of security for me. I had to realize if I was the one working, it was because God is providing. If Amy is the one working, it's because God is providing. If we both work, it's because God is providing. This was crucial for me and I hope as fathers you can understand who is really providing for your household.

Perhaps you are in the midst of a similar decision in your life where you or your spouse are considering if they should continue working. You might even be at the end of your career with retirement approaching. Can I take a moment to tell you no matter how much you worry about it, you'll always need God to provide? This doesn't mean to be foolish with your income or that poor decisions won't have consequences. I just want you to rest in the idea that whether or not you have two incomes in your house or are retiring from a career for thirty years, God is the one who provides.

If there is ever a moment where you think you are the one who did everything to support your family, you are wrong. God provided everything. He provided the skills you had. He provided the jobs you had. He provided your health along the way. He provided others to help you when you needed it.

As fathers, we feel responsible for providing the things our families need. This is a constant tension many of us wrestle with daily. Remind yourself that God is the provider and you should be thankful to be used by him.

WANTING TO BE A FATHER

In Genesis chapter 12, we read about a man named Abram who was living in a land called Haran. At the time Abram was seventy-five years old and without any children, including a son to be his heir. Abram desperately wanted to be a father. He was now an old man and the idea of becoming a father seemed impossible.

As we look at the following story, think back on your fatherhood journey. What was it like as you were trying to have a child? Do you remember waiting and wondering if it would ever happen? If you had trouble conceiving, how did this affect your relationship with God? Were you angry? Were you patient? How long did you wait? What matters is how God shaped you through this process and how you use it to share his goodness with others.

If you're now a father, was it through another means of fatherhood like adoption or fostering a child? There are many avenues to fatherhood and God can use them all for his glory. God gives us the gift of fatherhood in various ways. His plan is good. We just have to pay attention. Regardless of your fatherhood journey, God has been with you through all the ups and downs. God was with Abram, too. Let's see how fatherhood played out for him. This story is about how our Heavenly Father provided for Abram, and how he provides for each of us, too.

FATHER ABRAHAM HAD MANY SONS

In Genesis chapter 12, The Lord told Abram to go from his country into a land that he would show him and he would make him into a great nation. How did Abram respond to God's call? "So Abram went, as the Lord had told him..." (Genesis 12:4). I want to take a moment to understand Abram's attitude to God's call. While the verse is rather short, it has everything we need to understand Abram's attitude toward God. Read the verse again, it says, "So Abram went, as the Lord had told him."

Do you see Abram asking God for more clarity on what's going to happen? Do you see Abram waiting on more details? What about this great nation you're speaking of? How will this take place or even when? What kind of nation will this be? It's easy for us as fathers to want to see the entire plan upfront. We have our family's interests in mind but there are times when God is simply going to ask you to trust him without knowing the full plan. Will you listen?

Abram simply trusted and obeyed. He didn't demand more information or question how God would follow through on his promise. As a father, there are times in life when the outcome will be unclear. You won't know what to do and you may not even understand why. If you believe God is a good father, and we have seen he is, you'll have nothing to fear but you may have to wait. "Trust in the LORD with all your heart, and lean not on your own understanding" (Proverbs 3:5). Abram trusted God. If he had leaned on his own understanding, he would have missed all God was going to do through him. Ok, let's get back to the story.

Abram set off to the land of Canaan, he took all that they had including his nephew Lot, his wife Sarai, and all the people they had acquired in Haran. "Now there was a famine in the land…" (Genesis 12:10). This is the first trial we read about on his journey. As fathers, we experience trials all the time. Sometimes it is financial or illness. It might even be the loss of a job or loved one. When trials come, it's easy to lose hope, but never take your eyes off your Heavenly Father during difficult times.

We can all relate to Abram. God told Abram he would make him into a great nation but shortly after their journey started, they were in a tough spot. Something unexpected occurred and now Abram had a decision to make. Do I trust God and keep going or do I go my own way? When you're traveling alone, food is an issue, but when you have a large group of people to feed, a lack of food is a real problem. As a father, do you give up when things get tough or do you trust God and keep moving forward?

Because of the famine, Abram set off to Egypt in hopes he could find food for his people. When he entered Egypt, he told Sarai to tell the Egyptians she was his sister in hopes they wouldn't kill him as Sarai was very beautiful. They took Sarai into Pharaoh's house and Pharaoh gave Abram livestock as a gift. Abram's possessions grew greatly and then the Lord stepped in to help. The Lord was going to use Sarai later on in the story so he needed her back with Abram. The Lord afflicted Pharaoh's house with great plagues because of Sarai and shortly after, Pharaoh released them both and sent them on their way.

Later on in the chapter, Abram asks God a question. "But Abram said, "O Lord GOD, what will you give me, for I continue childless, and the heir of my house is Eliezer of Damascus?" (Genesis 15:2). Then the Lord told Abram, "...This man shall not be your heir; your very own son shall be your heir" (Genesis 15:4). As an old man, I'm sure this was almost impossible for Abram to believe. When we started this story Abram was seventy-five years old, can you imagine being a new father at seventy-five? Well, as strange as this sounds, Abram trusted God. "And he believed the Lord..." (Genesis 15:6).

In chapter 16, we learn Abram and Sarai are still without a child. Sarai tells Abram to go into her servant Hagar so that he may have children through her. This is another pivotal moment in the story. This is a moment where we can reach out and grab the "steering wheel" in the journey God has us on, or we can continue to trust and wait. In fatherhood, sometimes the only thing you can do is pray and wait.

Abram does have a child with Hagar named Ishmael. This, however, creates tension and jealousy between Sarai and Hagar. We see this tension occur and it's evident when we try to do things our way, we stand to make a mess of what God is doing in our life. Even though Hagar was not the son God was going to use to make Abram into a great nation, the Lord continues to provide for Abram.

It goes on to say, "When Abram was ninety-nine years old the LORD appeared to Abram and said to him, "I am God Almighty; walk before me, and be blameless" (Genesis 17:1). This is hard to imagine, right? Abram is almost one hundred years old! We started this journey when he was seventy-five and now almost twenty-five years later he still doesn't have the son God has promised him. As a father, how long have you waited on God for an answer to something in your life? Perhaps you're still waiting. How has the waiting shaped you as a father?

Most people are not very patient. We lead busy lives and live in a world of instant gratification. If you want to buy something, you can pull out your phone. Want to listen to music? You can stream it. Hungry? Just pop something in the microwave. Waiting twenty-five years to have the son God promised would have been hard. How would you have handled it? How would you have led your wife through this time? Would you have become discontent and cynical with God, or would you have taught those around you to wait on the Lord, knowing his timing is perfect? Next time you ask God for something and it hasn't happened by the weekend, remember,

Abram waited twenty-five years and still didn't have the son he was promised.

A NEW IDENTITY

In chapter 17, God changes Abram's name to Abraham. This is a very important detail and something we'll see throughout the Bible. The changing of his name symbolized how God transformed him into a new person. If you remember in the New Testament, he gives new names to others representing their new identity, too. Remember how Simon was later called Peter, or how Saul became Paul? This is the same transformation. When God changes you, you're a new person. The old man has died. God was making Abram a new person and going forward he would be called Abraham.

YOU WANT ME TO WHAT?

Has God ever asked you to do something and immediately you thought, "Um, are you serious?" While I'm sure there have been some difficult requests you've been asked to do in your life, I'm not quite sure you've had the same level of request as God asked Abraham. In verse 10, God asks Abraham to establish his covenant with him through circumcision. I would imagine most of us in this position would have at first been silent, paused to reflect on what we thought was said to us, and respond with, "You want me to what? ...Ugh, where?"

How about something else, God? What about a tattoo? You know, tattoos are in right now. Have you seen the guys from

Lot's tribe? That's some good ink. What if we get rid of beards? We'll switch completely to mustaches but no goatees. Will that work? How about no sandals? We'll institute no sandals on Saturdays. Yes, all sandals will be banished on Saturdays and this will be good enough, right? Nope.

This was going to be difficult and painful, to say the least. They didn't live in a society with modern medicine. They weren't able to numb the skin before the procedure or get some topical ointments at the store to make this process any easier. No, this was going to hurt.

While the request may seem rather difficult, this was part of the point. The idea was to follow God and trust his plan. Following God will cost you. Right now, following God was going to cost them something very personal; something which seemed hard to believe. As we'll see in this story, later on in Chapter 17, Abraham circumcised not only everyone in his household, his servants, but himself. At ninety-nine years old, Abraham circumcised himself in obedience to God (Genesis 17:24). When you think you're following God's direction in your life as a father, you start to see how a guy like Abraham sets the bar pretty high.

GOD KEEPS HIS PROMISES

After this long journey, in chapter 21 God keeps his promise to Abraham and gives him a son named Isaac. It would be through Isaac that God would keep his promise and make Abraham into a great nation. The journey had been long and hard. Over twenty-five years of waiting, but God is good and his timing is perfect. During this time God wasn't silent with Abraham, but used this time to build him into the man God wanted him to be. He was shaping him into the father he wanted him to be. He changed him into a new person and now Abram was Abraham, and Abraham was a father with the son God promised him.

Fathers, God wants to change you into the man he wants you to be. Are you listening to God and watching him transform you? God speaks to us through his word and the prompting of the Holy Spirit. If you're not reading his word, it's going to be hard to hear his voice. If you ever wonder why God sometimes waits before he answers a prayer of ours, it's because there are times when God needs to work on us before we are ready for what he has for us. Sometimes, this is a short period, and sometimes, like Abraham, it's years. God knows what is best and his timing is perfect.

GOD PROVIDES

When Titus was born, I remember standing in the hospital only moments after he was delivered and thinking, wow, this is my son! I was completely overjoyed with the gift God had given us and I instantly fell in love with this little guy. Do you remember the moment you first held your child? I bet you do. How did it make you feel? Do you remember the details of the day or does it all seem like a blur?

Abraham is now a father and you can imagine how much he loved Isaac. In chapter 22, God says, "...Take your son, your only son Isaac, whom you love, and go to the land of Moriah, and offer him there as a burnt offering on one of the mountains of which I shall tell you" (Genesis 22:2). After everything Abraham had been through to get a son, God asked him to sacrifice Isaac. How does he react? As a father, how would you react? Abraham did what he had been doing from the beginning, he trusted God. "So Abraham rose early in the morning, saddled his donkey, and took two of his young men with him, and his son Isaac. And he cut the wood for the burnt offering and arose and went to the place of which God had told him" (Genesis 22:3).

Once he arrived, he took Isaac and they walked up to where he would offer the sacrifice. Isaac asked, "...where is the lamb for a burnt offering?" (Genesis 22:7). Abraham responded, "God will provide for himself the lamb..." (Genesis 22:8). Abraham built the altar and placed Isaac on it, he then took the knife to sacrifice his son. Then the angel of the Lord appeared to Abraham and told him to not lay a hand on the boy. Instead, there was a ram caught in a thicket by his horns. God knew Abraham feared and trusted him and provided the sacrifice for Abraham instead of his son Isaac.

As a father, can you imagine the idea of being asked to sacrifice your child? The emotional pain this would cause is hard to imagine. Earlier in the chapter, it says it was a three day journey. I can't imagine the weight Abraham carried as he spent those few days with his son.

Does this story remind you of another one in the Bible? This story is a picture of God providing the ultimate sacrifice by giving his one and only son Jesus as a sacrifice on the cross for us. "He who did not spare his own Son, but gave him up for us all—how will he not also, along with him, graciously give us all things?" (Romans 8:32 NIV). God is a father who provides for his children and he has done so in the most magnificent way. We didn't deserve this provision and there is nothing we could have done to earn it.

There are going to be hard days in life when your fatherhood journey seems too much. There will be days when you feel like nothing is going right and the weight of the world feels to be on your shoulders. You might even have dark moments where you feel like the only decision you have is to leave. A father who provides for his family is a picture of how our father God provided for us. God hasn't just provided for us through Jesus but he continues to provide for us every day.

Our lives are filled with God's provision. Each breath and every heartbeat is a gift from God. I had a youth pastor growing up who would ask us to take a deep breath and say, "That was a good one." How true is this? Everything we have is from God. "For we brought nothing into the world, and we cannot take anything out of the world" (1 Timothy 6:7).

It's easy in our society to focus on what we don't have instead of what we do have. Our lives are too often filled with trying to keep up with those around us. Who has the biggest house or nicest car? Who went on the best vacation? The world wants to teach your children they must have the best of these things to be content. It's not true in your life and it's not true in theirs.

Few things in life are more transparent than discontentment. It's a cancer that spreads and suddenly nothing you have will be good enough. Many sins are less public but the struggle with discontentment is something that affects those around you. As a father, don't teach your family to chase the material possessions of life. Scripture says to build things that are eternal, not temporal (Matthew 6:19-21). As a father, what eternal things are you teaching your family? How are you providing? If you're teaching them to follow the one who provides it all, you're on the right track.

QUESTIONS FOR FATHERS

1. How has God provided for you over the years?
2. How long did your fatherhood journey take and what did it teach you about God's timing?
3. What is an area of your life you can trust God through that seems uncertain?

PRAYER FOR FATHERS

Pray and thank God for his provision over your household.

5

A FATHER PROTECTS

There are two kinds of parents in the world. The first type is what I like to call the "anti-risk" group. They wrap their entire home in bubble wrap to protect their child from the likely event of a fall. Their biggest fears in life are coffee table corners, electrical outlets, and let's not forget the dreaded stairs. They'll stop at nothing to avoid a sharp edge of any kind. You can recognize them as the parents that you see holding their child's hand as they walk into church together on Sunday morning.

Then you have the second type of parent that I like to call the "risk-ignorant" group. They live their lives seemingly unaware of any dangers. It's almost as if they have no children at all. You'll recognize them as the ones at church who need to stop mid-conversation with you to go find their child who ran off. Neither parent has it quite right but is striving to find the right balance of protection.

Another interesting behavior I've observed over the years is what I like to call the "law of many children." This law is as fundamental as Newton's laws of motion as you'll see in my next two examples. The law of many children states that as your number of children increases, your attention to any one child will decrease. In purely scientific terms, they have a direct correlation. Let me give you two examples before we move forward.

In the first example, you'll recount the number of pictures you have of your first child. They could likely fill a small private library. In contrast, the number of pictures you have of your next children starts to diminish. Typically the last child has about as many pictures as could fill a small fish bowl. Thus, the law of many children is validated.

For the second example, we'll use the name Henry for illustration purposes. If you only have one child and the church service is over, you'll say something like, "I'll get Henry." This shows your dedication to little Henry as you are taking ownership of the task.

Once you have a second child, you'll move to, "Do you want to get Henry?" This displays a passing of the responsibility to your wife. It doesn't display negligence of any kind but it does start to show the law of many children in motion.

Now, if you have three children, you might say, "Someone will get Henry." This could be your wife, perhaps one of your children, or maybe a parent from the anti-risk group who will bring your child to you. It could be any number of these outcomes.

Ok, now you've had your fourth child and things are more difficult. Once the church service is over, you'll probably say,

"Did anyone get Henry?" This displays that you as a parent have exceeded your mental capacity and better judgment with the fourth child. You're not a bad parent, just a very busy one.

If, somehow, you didn't get the hint that four children were enough, you might have made it to the final stage of the law of many children. In this stage, there is nothing anyone can do to help you other than pray for you. Once the church service gets out, you'll have made it all the way home before you say, "I don't think we got Henry." Thus, the law of many children has been validated.

OUR FATHER PROTECTS

As fathers, we naturally want to protect our children from harm but the reality is sometimes we can't. Our best efforts are not perfect and eventually, our child will get hurt. I remember as a new dad, anytime my children would get hurt, it would crush me. I didn't like to see the tears or scrapes they got along the way. Of course, it's a normal part of growing up and, thankfully, nothing was too bad.

As parents, we struggle to handle even the slightest sense of pain in our children. When our kids are sick, it's almost as if we are, too. We sit with them and take their temperature. We care for them and drive them to the doctor, if need be. We'll stop at nothing to protect our children and help them get better.

Have you ever taken time to stop and think about how God allowed his son to be crucified for you? As a father, this is a hard concept to understand. The Bible says, "But he was pierced for our transgressions; he was crushed for our iniquities; upon him was the chastisement that brought us peace, and with his wounds we are healed" (Isaiah 53:5).

I don't know of any fathers who would be willing to give up their son's life for another person, let alone for sinful people like you and me. However, the Bible says God did this very thing; "For one will scarcely die for a righteous person—though perhaps for a good person one would dare even to die—but God shows his love for us in that while we were still sinners, Christ died for us" (Romans 5:7-8). God did this very thing. He did it out of love but he also did it so we could have hope of an eternity spent with him.

Our Heavenly Father is a good father. Throughout scripture, he displays how he'll protect us when times get tough. He won't run away, and he'll be there, through the good and bad. If you're not resting on his promise of protection, can I ask you to stop and pray to him now? Look back on your life and I bet you'll see God's hand of protection over many situations.

Protection comes in many forms and can be reflected in several ways. Sometimes we pray for God's protection over our household. We desire for the safety of our family as we go about our activities each day. What a wonderful thing it would be to pray a quick prayer over your family each morning before everyone heads out the door.

In this chapter, we're going to look at the story of David. David needed protection from his Heavenly Father during a very difficult time. His attitude teaches us to trust God even when the outcome looks dire. As we'll see as we unpack the story, God protected David because he was going to use David in a mighty way. Many years later, Jesus would come from the line of David. It goes to show you how God is working a much larger plan than you may ever get to see with your own eyes. What's amazing about God is he chooses to use unlikely people to accomplish his plan. As a father, God wants to use you to serve your family in a mighty way. Will you let him?

JUST A SHEPHERD

Jesse the Bethlehemite had eight sons and David was the youngest in his family. The Bible says David was ruddy and handsome (1 Samuel 16:12). David was a shepherd and spent his days watching over the sheep of his household. While this doesn't seem like a big detail, God was using David during this time to shape him into whom he would need to be later on. David didn't know what the future held but he kept serving faithfully.

Have you ever felt like each day seems like the day before? Maybe you feel like you're not sure if you're living out your purpose. We all feel this way at times. There are times in life when what we're doing doesn't seem to make much sense. How can we be impactful by doing a job which seems so normal? It's likely David felt the same way, too. Each day his routine was probably pretty similar. As a shepherd, he would wake up early, feed the sheep, and watch over them throughout the day, ensuring none wandered off or were attacked. I'm sure most days were pretty similar. While this might seem insignificant, David was doing exactly what God needed him to do. Day in and day out, David was faithful and God was preparing him for more.

As a father, we sometimes forget how influential we can be to others around us. Are we building relationships? When was the last time you took someone a meal so they didn't have to cook? What about the last time you asked a coworker to lunch?

These might seem meaningless but if you don't reach out to those around you, you'll never be able to build a relationship and allow yourself the opportunity to serve. People want to see how a true father looks after those around him, and it's fun to get your family involved, too. I encourage you to think of someone you can bring dinner to this month. Maybe it's an elderly couple you know or someone who is sick. Prepare the meal together with your kids or pick up take-out and deliver it together. It's a great example to discuss how Jesus cares for others by using each of us.

Many times in life we view God's mission field as a faraway location like a third-world country. We seem to forget the lost and needy around us each day. You can be influential in the lives of those around you, especially your coworkers. How so, you might ask? Well, you likely spend more time with them than with your own family. This might seem shocking but if you take out the time you sleep, the work week usually ends up being more time than you spend at home. Do you have someone you could pick out at work to start building a deeper relationship with? Pray and ask God to put someone on your heart. Let's get back to David.

In verse 14, we learn the Spirit of the Lord has departed from King Saul and a harmful spirit is now tormenting him. It goes on to say, "'...See, an evil spirit from God is tormenting you. Let our lord command his servants here to search for someone who can play the lyre. He will play when the evil spirit from God comes on you, and you will feel better'" (1 Samuel 16:15-16 NIV). One of his servants remembered David and his abilities. Saul called for his servants to bring David to him. David became Saul's armor-bearer and played the lyre whenever Saul was being tormented by the spirit. God is already using David but he's not done with him yet.

GOLIATH OF GATH

In chapter 17, we learn the Philistines gathered their armies for battle. Saul and his army also gathered in preparation to fight. One day, a Philistine named Goliath of Gath came out to taunt the army of Israel. The Bible says his height was six cubits and a span. According to biblical scholars, this is roughly equivalent to nine feet tall. Goliath stood and shouted to the ranks of Israel asking them to send someone to fight him. If they were able to kill Goliath, the Philistines would surrender. But if Goliath won, the Isrealites had to surrender to them.

"When Saul and all Israel heard these words of the Philistine, they were dismayed and greatly afraid" (1 Samuel 17:11). Can you imagine being a part of the army of Israel and praying you won't be the one who is sent to fight Goliath? He's a giant and is ready to crush anyone who thinks they can take him. No one was willing to go fight him and they all felt there was no chance of a victory.

This is the moment when fear starts to enter the lives of Saul and his army. If there is one thing to know about fear, remember the following – fear is in opposition to God.

Throughout scripture, God asks us to trust him. While fear is a normal part of life, fear tugs at us to take our focus off God and place it on ourselves. What do you fear most as a father?

"For God hath not given us the spirit of fear; but of power, and of love, and of a sound mind" (2 Timothy 1:7 KJV). Fear is the enemy of faith. No matter the situation you're facing right now, God is with you through it all. Life is hard. There are going to be some really painful trials in your life. If you wake up each day to face uncertainty with fear, you'll be playing right into the devil's hand. You'll be back in the garden and being told you can't trust God. However, if you wake up and trust God amid uncertainty, you'll build a bridge for others to see Jesus. Fear says, "I can't trust God." Fear says, "God can't help me." Faith says, "I will trust God even when I cannot see." As we move forward, you'll see fear wouldn't be found in David, and it shouldn't be found in you.

For forty days, Goliath came forward to taunt the army of Israel and for 40 days no one would accept his challenge. I would imagine each day would feel like a slow death knowing eventually that Goliath won't wait any longer. Will it be today that he decides to come kill us or will it be tomorrow?

The Bible says during this time, David went back and forth between tending the sheep of his household and helping Saul. I don't want to pass over this part because I think it's a very significant detail. Listen up fathers – even though David was working with Saul, and even though his brothers were currently fighting a battle, David never lost sight of his original role to watch over the sheep.

Did you catch it? As fathers, there will be many things

happening all around us but we can never take our eyes off our calling from God to shepherd and love our family. We have a job to do and while the days might be hard, don't forget your purpose as a father. You are there to shepherd your household on both good days and bad ones. This is a great picture of how God watches over his sheep and is a reminder for us to remain steadfast when times get tough. What a wonderful God we serve.

Later on, David has come back to his brothers to see the latest in the fight with the Philistines. After watching Goliath once again taunt the army of Israel, David steps up and says, "...For who is the uncircumcised Philistine, that he should defy the armies of the living God?" (1 Samuel 17:26). David is saying, "Not today" and "Not in my house." This is the kind of faith fathers need. Remember how you're the door? Remember how it's your responsibility to watch over your wife and children? Do you want to know what a man who trusts God looks like? Look at David.

David told Saul, "...Let no man's heart fail because of him. Your servant will go and fight with this Philistine" (1 Samuel 17:32). David didn't care that Goliath was a giant. He didn't care that they had already been taunted for 40 days. He didn't think of all the ways that Goliath could kill him. All David knew was that Goliath was against his God, the only God.

Saul begins to attempt to talk David out of going to fight Goliath. He tells him that he's too young and how Goliath is a trained warrior. Here is another time when we can let fear creep into our lives. It's hard enough to get over our own doubting voice, but it's even harder when those surrounding us doubt our ability. As a father, there will be times when you'll think you're not cut out for this role or that you don't know enough. The truth of the matter is none of us are cut out to be fathers if we go at it alone. If we go into the battle of fatherhood trusting God like David, God will protect us.

When Saul told David he wasn't prepared to fight Goliath, David told Saul about all the times he protected his sheep. There were times when he had to fight off lions and bears. There were even times when one of these predators would take off with one of the sheep and David would go after them. He would kill them and bring the sheep back to the herd.

For years, David cared for his sheep without a single hint of how God was preparing him for a future battle. God used this time to shape David into a mighty warrior and, now, David was ready to fight. If David hadn't been faithful as a shepherd, he wouldn't have been prepared to fight Goliath. Whenever you feel like your days as a father are useless, remember David.

Not only was David willing to go fight Goliath, he told Saul the following, "...The Lord who delivered me from the paw of the lion and from the paw of the bear will deliver me from the hand of this Philistine..." (1 Samuel 17:37). This is a picture of someone fully surrendered to God. The fight of David's life was about to go down and he didn't leave room for fear. In tough situations, do you say, "The Lord will deliver me" or "Will the Lord deliver me?" One says "I trust God" and the other asks "Can I trust God?"

Saul places his armor on David but it doesn't fit quite right and David decides to go into battle without it. I believe David throwing aside Saul's armor symbolizes not wanting to carry anything into battle which would place his reliance on anything but the Lord. He throws his own safety net aside and has no one to rely on but God alone. This is an amazing picture of how we should toss aside our own false sense of security to let God fight our battles. David picks up five stones and walks into the fight of his life.

When Goliath saw David coming to the battle line, he taunted him for being just a young man. Goliath said he would feed his flesh to the birds. David responded, "...For the battle is the Lord's, and he will give you into our hand" (1 Samuel 17:47). Goliath made his move and headed straight for David. Without hesitation, David ran toward him. He could have turned around and said, "This was a bad idea," but instead he moved forward. David took out one of his stones and slung it toward Goliath with his slingshot. It hit Goliath straight in the forehead and he dropped over dead. This is like a boxing match where the bell goes off to start round one and it's a TKO. One shot and it was over.

For 40 days, this giant had tormented the army of Israel. It was the youngest son of Jesse the Bethlehemite, a shepherd no less, who took him down. No man in the army of Israel was willing to even try. David ran over to Goliath's dead body, took out Goliath's own sword, and cut off his head. This was a picture for everyone to see it was officially over. Goliath wasn't coming back. He was dead, and the Bible says the Philistines fled.

It's typical for men to enjoy a good battle scene. We feel the power of the moment and can almost taste the victory in which David prevailed. As fathers, we want to be like David and conquer the enemies of our household. We want to fight our own battles in life. This is a powerful story but if we left this story here, we would be missing an even bigger one.

Fathers, here's the deal, you're not David in this story. Jesus is David. He is the one who goes before us and fights our battles. He is the one who cut off the enemy's head when he died on the cross. He is the shepherd who is always watching over his sheep, and he is the one who protects us wherever we go. When David killed Goliath, this is a foreshadowing of Jesus crushing sin on the cross. If we go to battle by ourselves, we're going to lose, but if we go into battle with Jesus, we've already won.

The story of David is one of my favorites in all of the Bible. As a guitar player, I occasionally write songs. A few years ago, I wrote a song in response to this story. While you don't know the melody, I hope the words speak to you as much as they did to me. The song is called *Grace and Giants*.

The "one name" in this song is Jesus, and with him, all your giants can fall. Don't take your job as a father lightly. Don't let fear push out your faith. Our God is a protector of his children, and as a father, you are too.

Verse

I am weak but you're strong
Stronger than all of the voices I hear
Forty days is so long
Longer than I want to spend in my fear
No reason to hide
No reason to wonder if I'm growing old
Cause I'll rest when you're near
I'll rest when you're holding me straight through the storm

Chorus

You trade strength for my weakness
And you breathed life to my bones
One name when darkness surrounds me
Cause all of my giants can fall by your stones

QUESTIONS FOR FATHERS

1. What did you protect your children from this week?
2. How has God protected your household this year?
3. What false sense of security are you holding onto instead of God?

PRAYER FOR FATHERS

Pray and ask God to continue protecting your family.

6

A FATHER FORGIVES

As a father, teaching your children about forgiveness can be hard. You'll find yourself telling them, "You need to apologize." This is for two reasons. First, you want your child to recognize they have hurt someone, and second, you want them to apologize to the other person for their actions. The first part is obvious to most offenders as everyone generally knows when they have done something wrong. They sense the tension and broken fellowship which now exists. The second part is where things get hard. We simply don't like to admit we've done something wrong. We're ok with knowing we have, but we're not interested in admitting it.

The Bible speaks about how much impact our words have in the book of James. It compares the tongue to the rudder of a ship. The rudder is the small mechanism on the back that steers the ship in the direction it will go. The rudder on a ship is generally out of sight but this small feature controls everything. It's just like our tongue. Our tongue is a small feature in relation to our body but it allows us to produce the words we have each day.

Here's an example of how powerful words are and how much they make an impression in our minds. Think about a time when you argued with someone. This might have been a spouse, child, friend, or even a coworker. I'm sure you remember the harmful words exchanged. However, I bet you can't remember what either of you were wearing. Why? Words are more powerful.

James goes on to say, "...How great a forest is set ablaze by such a small fire!" (James 3:5) and this imagery is exactly how we see it in our life. You know the moment that a conversation turns into an argument, and a single word can, at times, be like throwing a match into a brush pile. It sets the whole forest on fire and it all starts with our words.

James says, "but no human being can tame the tongue. It is a restless evil, full of deadly poison" (James 3:8 NIV). We are all guilty of saying hurtful things. There have even been times when we know the exact wrong thing to say in the heat of the moment and choose to say it anyway. What I love about the Bible is the truths inside are as valuable today as they were thousands of years ago. I don't have to worry about waking up one day to realize this message is out of date. It's unchanging, just like our God.

James gives us a harsh reality check, he says, "With the tongue we praise our Lord and Father, and with it we curse human beings, who have been made in God's likeness" (James 3:9 NIV). This is a mic-drop moment. When you hear this passage you can't say anything because you know it's true. You simply feel the weight of these two realities. Do you wake up in the morning to read your Bible and then yell at your children? Do you serve at church but stir the pot of office gossip? If you own a business, how would your employees think your words compare to your testimony? Would there be a conflict? Anyone can look good in a corporate email, that's easy. The real question is how one would say you treat them behind closed doors. Do your words build a bridge to Jesus, or do they tear it down?

As a father, and especially as a man, I think we struggle with anger often. I'm not sure why but I feel all men seem to struggle with pride and anger at some level. One of the worst traits we can have in life as a father is an attitude where we don't show forgiveness. This is evil. Let me say it again – a lack of forgiveness is evil. Do I need to say it a third time?

A lack of forgiveness is evil because it goes against everything Jesus has done for us. An unforgiving heart is the anti-Gospel. Do you know what the Gospel means? It means the good news. Do you know what a lack of forgiveness means? It means very bad news because if we didn't have forgiveness through Jesus, it would indeed be very bad news. There is nothing more self-righteous than a lack of forgiveness. It tears down the bridge like nothing else.

Do you want to tell people about a God who forgave their sins, but you don't want to go to ask for their forgiveness? You can't have it both ways. Do you want to tell your kids what they did was wrong, but you won't apologize for what you said yesterday? You can't have it both ways. Do you remember the

Pharisees? Do they remind you of anyone at times? I'm looking at you and me.

There are so many stories in the Bible we could look at about forgiveness but we are going to look at just two. The first is about an actual father and his son. If you have a son you might be able to relate to this story, but it will be just as true for daughters, too. Pause right now and close your eyes, take time before you keep reading to ask yourself if you show a lack of forgiveness. If you're part of God's family, you can't be someone who shows a lack of forgiveness. You can't have it both ways.

THE PRODIGAL SON

In Luke chapter 15, we read about a man who had two sons. The younger son asked his father for his share of the property. His father gave him his portion and then the son left a few days later. The idea of inheritance is seen all throughout scripture. While these first two verses are short, I don't want to miss what the past might have been. His father likely worked hard his entire life to build up some form of inheritance for his sons. I don't want to diminish this idea. It's likely his father toiled, day after day, and saved to build something he could later leave his children. The son took his inheritance, and in the next verse, it says he squandered it in reckless living. What may have taken his father his entire life to acquire was lost in a moment. Everything was gone.

Shortly after this, a famine arose in this country and the son began to be in need. Since he didn't have any money, he took a job feeding pigs. If you've ever been to a farm that has pigs, you realize it's probably the most disgusting animal on the farm. Have you ever heard the saying, "This place is a pigsty"? This is why.

One of the reasons pigs are so messy is they don't sweat as we do. They must rely on the cool mud to keep their bodies from getting too hot. They roll around in the mud and this, of course, makes their entire area disgusting. "And he was longing to be fed with the pods that the pigs ate, and no one gave him anything" (Luke 15:16).

The son who was living under the shelter of his father's roof at the beginning of the story was now broke and desiring to eat the pig's food. This is quite the life change. He lost everything and didn't even have something to eat. He remembers that even his father's servants had something to eat, but here he was without anything. The son decides to go back to his father and tell him the following, "...Father, I have sinned against heaven and before you" (Luke 15:18). Does this seem like a self-righteous attitude? It doesn't to me. He goes on to say, "I am no longer worthy to be called your son. Treat me as one of your hired servants" (Luke 15:19). What do you think the father will do when his son returns home without any of his inheritance left? What would you have done if you took from your life savings and your son brought back nothing?

I bet most of us would be furious and begin to tell him what an awful job he did with what he was given. We would probably say, "Do you know how hard I worked for that?" I'm sure many of us have exploded on our children for much less than losing their inheritance.

Here is what the father did in the Bible – "And he arose and came to his father. But while he was still a long way off, his father saw him and felt compassion, and ran and embraced him and kissed him" (Luke 15:20). Before the son could even open his mouth, the father welcomed him home with open arms. He hugged and kissed him without a single word asking what he had done with the money he was given. The father called his servants to bring the best robe and prepare the fattened calf. He said, "...let us eat and celebrate" (Luke 15:23). In verse 24 it says, "'For this my son was dead, and is alive again; he was lost, and is found.' And they began to celebrate" (Luke 15:24).

With Jesus, we don't get second best, we get the best. The father didn't ask for an old sweatshirt and chicken wings, he asked for the best robe and the fattened calf. Our Heavenly Father forgives us and welcomes us whenever we admit we messed up. He doesn't berate, but embraces. He forgives and prepares a table before us. There is no lack of forgiveness in this story and there is no lack of forgiveness with God. "Be kind to one another, tenderhearted, forgiving one another, as God in Christ forgave you" (Ephesians 4:32). Fathers, we forgive because he first forgave us.

This story is a picture of how Jesus welcomes those who go astray and come back to him. When we hurt someone, or are hurt by someone, we must forgive or ask for forgiveness. "If we confess our sins, he is faithful and just and will forgive us our sins and purify us from all unrighteousness" (1 John 1:9 NIV). Forgiveness is a picture of the perfect father.

There will be times when your children come home dreading your reaction to their mistakes. The teenage years can especially be hard. What if your son comes home drunk, or what if your daughter comes back three hours after her curfew? Instead of meeting them at the door with harsh words, what if you opened the front door with open arms? This would be a better picture of Jesus. I'm not saying there isn't a time to discuss what happened and discipline your child. As we'll learn later, discipline is love. If you don't discipline, you don't love your child. What I'm asking is to consider how Jesus welcomes us when we come back to him.

FEED MY SHEEP

At the beginning of the Gospels, we see a group of men fishing. They aren't having much luck and they are about to call it a day. Suddenly, Jesus asks them to toss their nets over the side of the boat. At first, they hesitate because they have been at it all night with nothing to show, but decide to do as he said. Their nets became so full of fish that they were breaking when they tried to pull them back into the boat. One of these fishermen was Simon (who would later be named Peter). Out of all the disciples, James, John, and Peter were closer to Jesus than any of the rest throughout his ministry. This gave them a special relationship and a vantage point that none of the others had.

When we think of the disciples, many of us might picture people who were very qualified to serve the Lord. We might think of highly educated people who had their lives in order. If you're only going to pick twelve disciples, doesn't it make sense to pick the smartest people you can find? While you might have the image of theologians following Jesus, nothing could be further from the truth.

The group of men who followed Jesus throughout his ministry would be about equivalent to the last ones picked in gym class. They were all from various backgrounds and didn't have any sense of notoriety to their name. During the time they were with Jesus, they were able to witness firsthand the miraculous events Jesus demonstrated throughout his ministry. They watched Jesus give sight to the blind, heal leprosy, make the lame walk, exorcize demons, feed thousands of people with just a few fish, turn water into wine, and the list goes on and on.

Having witnessed these events, it gave them a relationship with Jesus unlike anyone else in scripture. Their loyalty to Jesus was deeper than could be described in words. In the Garden of Gethsemane, Peter was the one who pulled out a sword to fight the men who came to arrest Jesus. He was a protector.

The night before Jesus was crucified, Jesus tells the disciples that they will all fall away that night. He says the sheep will be scattered. Peter speaks up and says, "...I will never fall away" (Matthew 26:33). Jesus tells Peter, not only will you fall away but before the rooster crows, you will deny me three times. Peter responds, "Even if I must die with you, I will not deny you!" (Matthew 26:35).

In just a few hours Peter would do exactly as Jesus said. Once Jesus was arrested and taken by the guards, Peter followed closely behind him as they carried him away. While Jesus was being interrogated, Peter stood in the courtyard watching from a distance. Three different individuals asked Peter if he knew Jesus and all three times he said he didn't. On the last denial, Peter heard a rooster crow. He remembered what Jesus had told him and then the Bible says he wept bitterly (Matthew 26:75).

Peter didn't have another opportunity to speak with Jesus before he was crucified. He didn't get a chance to apologize or beg Jesus to forgive him. After all that Peter and Jesus had gone through, Peter's last interaction was a denial of the one he loved. Not only was it denial, but the Bible says Jesus and Peter locked eyes when he denied him for the third time (Luke 22:61). What a crushing weight this must have been for Peter.

In John chapter 21, the disciples were back to their old job. They were once again fishing and they weren't having much luck. They heard a voice from the shore telling them to toss their nets over the other side of the boat and once again their nets were so full they couldn't haul it in. Peter immediately recognized it was Jesus and jumped out of the boat into the water. When he got to the shore Jesus had a fire and made breakfast for them.

In this chapter, Jesus said to Peter, "When they had finished breakfast, Jesus said to Simon Peter, 'Simon, son of John, do you love me more than these?' He said to him, 'Yes, Lord; you know that I love you.' He said to him, 'Feed my lambs' (John 21:15). Jesus asked Peter the question a second time. Peter responded again, "Yes, Lord you know I love you" (John 21:16). Jesus responded, "Tend my sheep" (John 21:16). A third time Jesus asked Peter the same question. Peter responded, "Lord, you know everything; you know that I love you" (John 21:17). Jesus said, "Feed my sheep" (John 21:17).

Right here is true fatherhood. Peter has been wrecked for

weeks about the three times he denied Jesus and what does Jesus do when he sees Peter? Does he start laying into him about how much of a disappointment Peter is and how he's not fit to be a disciple? Does he start telling Peter how James and John would have never done this to him? No, instead Jesus says, "Feed my sheep."

Jesus knows Peter messed up. Peter knows he messed up. Peter is crushed by what he did to Jesus. Instead of Jesus rubbing salt in Peter's wounds, he tells him to get back to work, to get back to the mission. Jesus told them they would become fishers of men and Jesus said he needed to get back at it. Did you notice how many times Jesus asked Peter if he loved him? Three times. This was the number of times Peter denied him. I love these details in scripture.

As fathers, our children will remember how we treat them when they have messed up. How we respond in these moments is crucial in pointing them to Jesus. Peter didn't deserve for Jesus to tell him to "Feed my sheep" but what a blessing it is to be the son of a Heavenly Father who doesn't give us what we deserve.

QUESTIONS FOR FATHERS

1. Who in your life do you need to forgive?
2. How can you teach your children to forgive others?
3. What is a recent situation where you did not show the forgiveness God has shown you?

PRAYER FOR FATHERS

Pray and ask God to help you forgive those who have hurt you.

7

A FATHER SERVES

It was the Spring of 2011 and my grandfather had just passed away. He was eighty-four years old at the time and I was just getting ready to graduate college. Grandfathers are wonderful. If you still have a grandfather in your life, don't take it for granted. Anytime you have an opportunity, pull up a chair next to him and ask him to tell you about his life. Learn about his childhood and soak up any wisdom he'll share. If he's a believer, ask him to tell you what God has done for him. I love the wisdom and guidance of older men. I desire to grow old and share what Jesus has done for me with younger men.

I have so many fond memories of growing up and spending time with my grandparents. I remember as a kid, they would take us to the park to feed the ducks. I remember spending birthdays and Christmases together around great food and grandma's famous cookies. Spending the night at their house was fun because I got to do things my parents wouldn't let me do. Aren't grandparents great? I still miss him praying before a holiday meal together. It was the voice of a wise man who loved everyone well.

And while you leave most funerals grieving, I left my grandfather's with a mission. There was something that stuck out to me during his service that I won't ever forget.

A MODERN-DAY SERVANT

My grandmother was one tough lady. I remember when we arrived at the church for my grandfather's funeral, the first thing she did was hug us and say, "Let's go see grandpa." I can almost hear her voice because this moment reminded me of how strong she was in life. Her husband of sixty years had just passed away, but she was making sure we were all ok. She was a rock for all of us that day, especially during such a hard time for herself. I sure miss that lady.

The funeral service was especially impactful to me. I was two months away from asking Amy to marry me, and as my story with Amy was just beginning, I couldn't help but think my sweet grandmother's marriage had just ended. It was like seeing the bookends of life in one setting. It was surreal to me because I knew that one day, one of us would be right in her spot. Our entire life would fly by and death would eventually come.

During the service, the pastor said many wonderful things about his life. He served his family and church well. What more could you want in a father and grandfather? However, there was one specific story the pastor shared which I think about to this day.

The church my grandparents attended was the oldest in their county. The original church building is still standing and they use it for certain aspects of their church's ministry to this day. The pastor described how the original church has an old leaky basement. Whenever there was a storm with several inches of rain, the basement would flood. He went on to tell us he couldn't remember how many times my grandfather would gather up a group of men (including the pastor who was speaking) to go to the church and pump the water out of the basement so it would be usable for services on Sunday.

This story is the pinnacle of a modern-day servant. It's not a flashy story and wouldn't ever make the news. No, this is a story about a man who loved the Lord and taught other men to love him too. This is a story about how a father serves those around him. This is someone who needs no one to know he's spending his own time for the lives of others.

I'm sure there were people in the service on those Sundays after a storm who had no idea the effort these men put in earlier in the week so they could come and worship that morning. He did this and so many other things because he loved the Lord and knew what the Lord had done for him.

There have been several additions to the church since those days and their congregation has grown tremendously. A big service was 100 people when my mom was growing up and today the church has 600 in weekly attendance. It was always a joy to attend when I visited. Later on in college, I was fortunate enough to play a worship set in the original church building for one of their youth nights. It was a very special opportunity for me as I felt like I was able to be a part of my grandparent's faith journey as the next generation of their family.

My grandfather wasn't perfect, but I know the "bricks of faith" he laid at that church over the years built a bridge for others to see Jesus. There is a generation attending this church today who have no idea who my grandparents were. However, I know his servant's heart was used by God and his service will last for generations.

ARE YOU WILLING?

When we think about being a servant, there is no better picture than Jesus. His entire life was spent in service to his people. Everything Jesus did was out of love. Fathers, my question to you is this – are you willing to be used by God?

Being used by God can take many forms. Sometimes this is in simple acts of service over a lifetime. Sometimes it's through the ability to give financially in a way others can't. Sometimes it might even be with a trial.

While trials in life may not seem like a way you can point others to Jesus, you might not be looking at the bigger picture. Sometimes people get sick and unfortunately, sometimes they die. Do we wonder how anything like this can be good? How can God use such a moment of heartbreak for his kingdom when it leaves so many people grieving? We're going to look at a story about death and how God used a difficult time to bring others to him.

THE DEATH OF LAZARUS

In John chapter 11, we learn about a man named Lazarus of Bethany. Lazarus was the brother of Mary and Martha, and also a friend of Jesus. Mary was the one who anointed Jesus' feet with expensive perfume and wiped them with her hair.

We learn that Lazarus was ill. When you're a follower of Jesus, it makes sense to go ask for his help. So, that's exactly what they did. The sisters went to Jesus and told him "...he whom you love is ill" (John 11:3). This probably seems like a pretty small request from Mary and Martha. They have been with Jesus for some time now during his ministry and they have witnessed him do miraculous deeds. Jesus has healed many people, and since they have such a close relationship with him, it likely seemed to be a very small matter.

Jesus responds, "This illness does not lead to death. It is for the glory of God, so that the Son of God may be glorified through it" (John 11:4). It goes on to say Jesus loved Martha, Mary, and Lazarus. This is not a small detail. Fathers, when you are going through a trial in life, you must never think that God has abandoned you. He will never leave you.

I'm sure what happened next completely confused Mary and Martha. It says, "So, when he heard that Lazarus was ill, he stayed two days longer in the place where he was" (John 11:6). I know exactly what I would have thought. I would have said, "Um, what?" This is a pivotal moment for the sisters' faith. They have watched Jesus do things that have never been seen by anyone on the earth and when they make a request about their brother being ill, Jesus does nothing. What would you have done? How would this have affected your relationship with Jesus? As a father, when you pray for your children, spouse, or others, and nothing seems to happen, what do you think?

As far as Mary and Martha were concerned, Lazarus was going to die. Jesus had decided to stay where he was and there wasn't anything they could do. When Jesus finally came to where he was, Lazarus had already been dead for four days. Not only had Lazarus died of his illness, but he was already buried. Mary and Martha were in the middle of grieving and several Jews were comforting them. When Martha heard Jesus was coming, she went to meet up with him. "Martha said to Jesus, 'Lord, if you had been here, my brother would not have died'" (John 11:21). Martha is heartbroken that her brother had died. Not only is she upset, she still doesn't understand why Jesus let this happen.

However, in the following verse, she shows her faith in action. Even though she asked Jesus to heal her sick brother, even though Jesus didn't do so, and even though Lazarus died, she says, "But even now I know that whatever you ask from God, God will give you" (John 11:22). She is saying, "I still trust you even though I cannot see." How incredible is this?

Fathers, you can't just trust Jesus in the middle of a trial, you must trust Jesus on the other side too. The other side may be healing, but it may also be death. What will you do if you lose your wife? Will you still trust Jesus? What about if you lose a child? Will you still trust Jesus? Maybe you're wanting to be a father so bad but up to this point you've only had miscarriages. Will you still trust Jesus? Remember, Martha watched Jesus let her brother die. This was all she knew at the time but she trusted Jesus through it all. It doesn't mean she wasn't sad and it doesn't mean she wasn't confused. Grieving isn't a lack of faith. As we'll now see, it's normal, even for Jesus.

Martha ran to get Mary and when they came back to Jesus, she questioned his actions too. She felt crushed by what had taken place. It goes on to say that "Jesus wept" (John 11:35). Why did Jesus do this? I think there are a couple of reasons. First, Jesus truly loved Lazarus. It was the same feeling you had when one of your loved ones passed away. Death is sad, even for Jesus. Second, I think he was grieved because he was witnessing the effects of sin. Death entered the world because of sin. Once again, it all goes back to the garden. Jesus could likely remember all the times he had shared with Lazarus. Since sin introduced suffering into the world, Lazarus would be a victim of it too. Death is painful for both those in it and those watching it.

In just a short time, Jesus was going to go to the cross to end the power of sin forever. "O death, where is your victory? O death, where is your sting?" (1 Corinthians 15:55). Death may have had its moment for Lazarus, but it wouldn't forever. At present, Jesus was seeing this grim reality in someone he loved. Sin is destructive. It's deadly. Lazarus couldn't escape it on his own and neither can you.

Jesus asked, "...Where have you laid him? (John 11:34). He asked them to take away the stone in front of his tomb. They were perplexed and told Jesus there will be an odor as he has been dead for four days. They went ahead and took away the stone and Jesus lifted up his eyes and said, "...Father, I thank you that you have heard me. I knew that you always hear me, but I said this on account of the people standing around, that they may believe that you sent me" (John 21:41-42).

Did you see how Jesus prays? He acknowledges that his father always hears him. When we pray to God, he always hears us. Jesus calls on his Heavenly Father. Jesus goes right to the source of life itself. Then he cried out, "Lazarus, come out" (John 11:43). The Bible says the man who died came out. This dead man came back to life and a multitude of people were a witness to this extraordinary event.

The last part of this passage is where God's bigger plan is revealed in the story of Lazarus. It's the plan no one understood at the time and it's all summed up in a single verse, "Many of the Jews therefore, who had come with Mary and had seen what he did, believed in him" (John 11:45.) This entire trial, this illness, and death of a man, the brokenness of two sisters, and the confusion likely experienced, were all so that a group of people could witness this event and come to know Jesus. While Lazarus was brought back to life, the bigger story here is many of the witnesses went from death to life. Everything changed for a group of people that day and the faith of the two sisters built a bridge for others to see Jesus.

A father serves his children as we've seen in this story but it doesn't mean a father gives his children everything they ask for on their timetable. Our Heavenly Father is wise and knows what's best for us. We need to ask God for wisdom to know how to answer the requests of our children. Sometimes we'll give them what they ask for and sometimes we won't. If we want to be a father who serves his children, we must first look at the perfect father who serves us.

QUESTIONS FOR FATHERS

1. How are you serving your family?
2. How can you be more involved with your church?
3. How can you teach your children to serve like Jesus?

PRAYER FOR FATHERS

Pray and thank God for serving you through a difficult time in your life.

8

A FATHER HELPS

"Hey dad, can you help me get these legos apart?" Sure buddy, bring them here. "Hey dad, can you help me pick up my room?" You bet, bud. "Hey dad, would you help me get a snack?" Yeah, I'll get you one. "Hey dad, will you help me put on my superhero costume?" Yes, I will. "Hey dad, I need some help." Ok, I'm on my way.

Do any of the phrases sound familiar to you? As a father of young children, we hear these phrases all the time. While dads are busy themselves, I'm sad that there will be a day when I won't hear a little voice asking me for help with these simple matters. I'm not saying I've never been frustrated with "one more" request but I like knowing my kids need me. Do you remember your father helping you with similar tasks as a kid? What about a project you did together? I remember a specific one myself.

DON'T PASS ME THE BALL

When I was in middle school, I decided to try out for the basketball team. In retrospect, I'm not sure why. I hadn't played much basketball growing up and I was really more of a baseball player. However, I was determined to give it a try. Thankfully, there were no cuts at tryouts so anyone who wanted to play would make a team. When I say "a team," it's true. In the seventh grade, we had multiple teams based on skill set.

There was the "A" team which, as you could imagine, was generally the tall, athletic type. These players have been playing basketball since they could walk. They were typically in competitive leagues outside of school and were always wearing either Jordan or Iverson sneakers. They didn't only look the part but they really played well, too.

Then there was the "B" team, which was for players who didn't quite make the A team. They were still pretty good. Sometimes they even played up a team if there were A team players who couldn't make a game.

Finally, there was the "C" team. It was for players who played as well as you would expect kids who didn't make the other two teams. These players knew what a basketball was but that was about it. What team do you think I made?

You got it – I was a proud member of the glorious seventh-grade C team. In fact, not only was I on the C team but I was on the C2 team because there were too many students who wanted to play. We shared half of the games with the C1 team. I told myself C1 wasn't any better, but now I'm not sure that was true.

Anyway, I did get a pair of Iverson basketball shoes so I felt cool.

When you play seventh-grade C team basketball, you need a basketball goal at home to practice your game. I asked my parents if we could get a basketball goal and they, without hesitation, said yes. Looking back I'm not sure if their overly enthusiastic attitude to purchase a goal was due to their generous heart or my poor basketball skills. Either way, I was thrilled.

I remember going to pick out a basketball goal. I didn't know anything about them and neither did my parents. I said, "Can we get that one?" It had a fiberglass backboard which I thought looked like the ones NBA players used. Again, I felt cool. When you play C team basketball you need to feel cool as often as possible because when you step out on the court, you're quickly reminded how uncool you are in this sport.

We finally got the gigantic box home but still didn't have a goal. There was one large challenge ahead and it wasn't just my basketball season. It was to assemble the goal. My dad and I pulled it out of the box and it had 1,472,168 pieces. Not really, but it sure felt like it. I wasn't too overwhelmed because as a kid you don't have a sense of how much work goes into something. However, my dad had the face of someone who needed to figure out how to get the space shuttle back to earth with only the items he currently had in his pockets.

It didn't matter, we slowly but surely worked at putting it together. I think we worked on it every night for a week before we had something which mildly resembled a basketball goal. There were mechanisms, springs, hundreds of bolts, and washers. We built all of it inside our garage until we were finished. I felt like we were assembling an airplane inside of a hanger before it could take flight. Finally, the day had come. It was finished.

I want to take a moment to explain the two types of fathers when it comes to putting things together. Yes, all fathers can be summed up into two camps. The first type is the "don't over tighten the bolt" father. This father threads everything by hand first and then gently uses a wrench to give it a little twist to finish it off. He understands imported products can't take much force.

The second type is known as the "how tight can I get this" father. You know you have this father if you see furniture around your home with small cracks near where the bolts attach legs and other structural elements together. You will also notice bent metal on swing sets and bicycles. While I'm personally the first father in the scenario above, I'm still the proud son of the second type. Which father do you have?

Once we got it outside, it actually worked. We celebrated like two people who built the pyramids in Egypt. There was one more task that needed to be finished. If you've ever purchased a portable basketball goal, you know you typically fill them with water so the goal won't blow over in a storm. My father comes from the "anti-risk" parent group that we discussed in chapter five. Instead of water, he filled our goal with sand. It now weighed approximately 1,472,168 pounds. It never moved.

When we think about helping our children, you might have a similar story from your childhood where your dad helped you build a fort or science project. Fathers who help their children say with their actions, "I'm here for you" or "When you need anything, just let me know." Our Heavenly Father is no different. He's there for us when our earthly father is not. No matter how great your father is, he's not perfect. Let's see how a perfect father helps his children.

EVEN IF HE DOESN'T

Have you ever been to a concert at an outdoor amphitheater and sat in a crowd with thousands of other people? This is the best way I can describe the scene in the story we're about to look at. In Daniel chapter 3, we read about King Nebuchadnezzar. He is over all the land and everyone in it. During his reign, he decides to create a statue out of gold for all the people to worship. This is a huge statue and would be the centerpiece of the town. He tells the people that when they hear the sound of the music, they are to fall down and worship the golden image. If they don't, they will be thrown into a fiery furnace.

What if during the concert you were attending, the lead singer asked everyone in the audience to bow down to him? You, being a follower of Jesus, would think this seems wrong. However, you start looking around and every single person in the entire concert is bowing down except you and your two friends. I'm sure you would feel like all eyes were on you as you were still standing right in the middle of the crowd.

This is exactly what Shadrach, Meshach, and Abednego felt when they heard the music. There were people all around them but since they served God, they were unwilling to bow to this false god. It was brought to the attention of King Nebuchadnezzar that these three men would not bow down to his statue. He became furious and requested they be brought to him immediately. When they arrived, he asked them if what he was hearing was true. Could it be that they wouldn't bow down to his golden image?

They responded to King Nebuchadnezzar and said, "...King Nebuchadnezzar, we do not need to defend ourselves before you in this matter. If we are thrown into the blazing furnace, the God we serve is able to deliver us from it, and he will deliver us from Your Majesty's hand. But even if he does not, we want you to know, Your Majesty, that we will not serve your gods or worship the image of gold you have set up" (Daniel 3:16-18 NIV).

We can't overstate this story enough because it's a story that we will all face in our life in various ways. As fathers, we will be pressured to conform to the world and its ideals. We can choose to "bow down" or we can remain standing in submission to God. Sometimes, our submission to God is going to cost us. In this story, it appears like it might cost these guys their life. The last part of this passage is where we see true faith enter the picture. They know the King isn't bluffing. They not only have heard of the fiery furnace, but I'm sure they have even seen it themselves. Their faith is made evident when they say, "even if he does not."

Shadrach, Meshach, and Abednego fully believe God will help and save them from King Nebuchadnezzar. What's incredible about this story is their perspective during the trial. They are fully confident that God *can* save them but they don't know *if* God will save them. Don't miss this attitude, fathers. They are trusting God's plan even if they don't get the outcome they desire.

Whatever trial comes your way, know that God can help you. God can get you through it. God can save you. God can heal you. However, God may not do so. Does this make him bad? No, it makes him God. Fathers, if we believe God is above all and has our best interest in mind, we must believe he is working a much better plan than we can see. The question is, will you still serve him "even if he does not."

King Nebuchadnezzar was filled with rage and ordered the furnace to be heated seven times hotter than normal. He then had some men of his army throw Shadrach, Meshach, and Abednego into the furnace. The furnace was so hot it even killed the men whom King Nebuchadnezzar asked to carry out his orders.

Astonished, King Nebuchadnezzar noticed the men were not hurt but stood in the furnace unharmed. He ordered Shadrach, Meshach, and Abednego to come out of the furnace. They were completely unharmed and King Nebuchadnezzar believed in their God. He even established that anyone who didn't serve the God of Shadrach, Meshach, and Abednego would be killed.

God used the faith of Shadrach, Meshach, and Abednego to turn the King and the people who witnessed their acts of faith to him. They had no idea if God would save them. They believed he could but knew it might not happen. Trusting God can be difficult and when you're raising children in a world where peer pressure is challenging your authority, remember these guys and how they stood up for what they knew was right.

God loves to help his children. Helping our children is

something we should always be looking to do. You don't need to wait for your kids to ask for help, you should go ask them how you can help. A good father sees their child in need and goes to their aid before they ask.

Do you remember when your child took their first steps? Did they walk across the room on the first try? No, they took one step and then fell down. As a father, what did you do? You went over to pick them up. You didn't tell them how uncoordinated they were or that they didn't make it very far. No, you cheered them on because you're here to help them learn to walk. This is how God treats us too. He is there cheering us on every day. As fathers, he wants to help us love our families. He wants to help us protect our kids. He wants to help us provide for others. He wants to help us because he's a good father who helps his children.

My son Titus likes to play at the playground in our neighborhood. The playground has a rock wall and when he was little he wasn't strong enough to move up the wall on his own. I would hold him against the wall and with my help, he was able to move his feet to each mount and make it to the top. With each step he took, I had a hold of him. I wasn't going to let him fall and he trusted me to get him to the top.

Are you letting God help you make it through each day or are you trying to scale the wall on your own? If I was to let Titus climb on his own, he would have never made it. As fathers, we can choose to be in control or we can let God lead us through the fatherhood journey.

Titus is all boy. He's rough and loves to play with action figures. Over the last several months, Titus has brought me one of his toys to glue back together multiple times because his playtime has been too much for their plastic components. When he first brought me the broken toy, I told him, "It's ok buddy, I can help you." I took some super glue and with a little effort, we had it back in action to once again save the day. A few weeks later, Titus comes to me again with the same toy. How did I handle it? I had a moment where I wanted to say, "Buddy, you need to not be so hard on your toys. This is silly that you keep breaking it." While this wouldn't have been a wrong response, I felt like I needed to show him what Jesus does for us. I proceed to say, "Sure buddy, I can fix it again for you."

No matter how many times we come to Jesus with our problems, he is always there to help. He doesn't lead with anger or put us down. He loves to help us if we're willing to come to him. Don't ever stop helping your children no matter how old they get because our Heavenly Father never stops helping us.

QUESTIONS FOR FATHERS

1. When was the last time you helped your child with something important to them?
2. How can you show your children you're always available to help?
3. How can you teach your children to help others like Jesus?

PRAYER FOR FATHERS

Pray and ask God to help you spend more time with your children.

9

A FATHER PRAYS

If you want to look at a picture of an honest prayer life, look at the prayers of children. What is great about children praying is they are real and don't hold anything back. I think as adults we can struggle with prayer. What good does it do? Does God hear all of our requests? Does he even care? What about small requests? How do we know something will change?

If I'm being honest, prayer has been something I've struggled with during my life. Over the last year, I have taken the time to work on my prayer life as I've wanted to mature in this area. I think there has been a cynical part of me who wonders what the benefit is of prayer at times. I want to see an immediate result from anything I do. With prayer, results like this aren't always typical. As a father, can you relate?

When Titus turned two years old, we started praying before bedtime. He didn't actually pray quite yet, but Amy and I would pray before we tucked him in. This was a pretty simple routine at night and consisted of a very short prayer. It was nothing more than telling Titus that God loves him and likes to hear from him. Over time, Titus began to pray. At first, his prayers were all over the board, but they were honest. He would pray for items in his room like his bed or toys. It sounds silly but he was beginning to grasp the idea of being thankful.

We decided we wanted everyone to pray each night so we could model to Titus what it's like to pray. We wanted him to start hearing about some of the things we pray for too. We don't go very deep but we include both praises and requests. These might be thanking God for our day and also for helping someone feel better if they are sick. His prayers are starting to mature and it's exciting to watch his prayer life develop.

I don't want to give the impression we're killing it as parents. This would be inaccurate. We're trying to be proactive but many nights it's like pulling teeth. Some nights he's focused and other nights he's not very engaged. If you're starting to work on praying with your kids, know that this is normal. I'll share a funny story of a recent prayer from Titus.

About a week ago, it was my birthday. We were tucking Titus into bed and ready to pray like we do every night. We asked Titus, "What are you going to pray about tonight?" He sat and thought about it. After enough silence had passed, Amy prompted him and said, "Do you want to thank God for Daddy's birthday?" He said ok. Then he started to pray. "Dear God, thank you for letting us have steak tonight. Amen." I felt a little slighted but I quickly got over it. To be fair, the steak we had for dinner was pretty good.

THE PAUSE BEFORE PRAYER

When do you pray? Do you pray together as a family before meals? If so, why? I think for most people praying together before meals is a common time of prayer they have in their life. Have you ever thought about *why* you do it? It's not because you're trying to prevent the food from making you sick. Praying for our meals is a moment where we can pause and direct our thanks to the provider, God. He is the one who has allowed this meal in our life and we want to thank him for his continued provision. It's a blessing to pray.

The pause we take before we pray is a significant moment in our faith. It doesn't matter if we're praying for food or the healing of a loved one. What lasts for a millisecond is a transfer of trust and acknowledgment of our need for God. When we stop to pray, we're saying, "I can't do this alone." We move from a reliance on ourselves to a position of resting in him. The pause we take before a moment of prayer is a look into our heart. If we don't take time to pray, we're saying, "we've got everything under control." Except the reality is we don't.

What are some occasions in your life when you pray? Do you have a quiet time in the morning where you read the Bible and pray? Do you pray in the car on your way to work? When was the last time you prayed this week? As I've grown as a father, I think the best thing I can do for my kids is to pray. I can't be everything to them. I can't be a perfect dad. I can however pray to a perfect Heavenly Father who can help them in ways I can't.

ANSWERS TO PRAYER

Prayer can challenge our faith because we may not get the answer we want. If someone is sick in your life, you might naturally pray for this person. You might even pray for them for months or even years. What happens if this person dies? Did God not hear you? Does God not care? It's important to know how God answers prayers. He will answer them with yes, no, or not at this time. Let's look at each of these outcomes.

First, God may answer your prayer with a yes. You can pray for someone to be healed and it may happen. Let's say you're praying for a friend who has cancer. After several months of treatment, they go into remission and are declared cancer free. This is a moment to celebrate. Praise the Lord for his goodness!

Second, God may say no. Let's use the same scenario. You pray daily for this friend but after a tough battle, they pass away. You would praise God in the first situation but what about this one?

Lastly, God can answer with not at this time. This answer can be hard because to us, it appears as a no. There is no immediate change in the situation we are praying for and, therefore, we can lose hope. When God answers prayer with no or not at this time, you have a decision to make. You can trust that God is sovereign even though you don't understand, or you can assume prayer doesn't work. I think we all too often think prayer doesn't work but what is happening is that God answered us with one of these last two outcomes. Does this seem like it could be true for you?

JESUS MODELS PRAYER

In scripture, Jesus models how we should pray and the Lord's prayer is a great framework. In Matthew 6:9-13 NIV, Jesus goes through a model of prayer for us. In this prayer, he addresses God as *our father*. Jesus knows everything he has comes from the father and this is how our attitude should be in prayer too.

He goes on to say, "your kingdom come, your will be done." This is the part of our prayer we often leave out. We don't want an outcome that goes against our desires but if we believe God is good, we need to trust him. God's will may not be healing. God's will may not be the new job. God's will may not be starting a business. God's will may be different from your will. If his will is different from your will, are you going to trust his decision?

He goes on to say, "give us this day our daily bread." Jesus knows where all of his meals come from. He then says, "And forgive us our debts, as we also have forgiven our debtors." Jesus lived a perfect life and didn't have anything which needed to be forgiven. He is simply modeling for us how our attitude should be toward God. We constantly need God's forgiveness because we all mess up daily. We also need to be quick to forgive others just like he forgives us. It finishes with, "but deliver us from the evil one." This is a closing statement for God's protection over our life.

This prayer is a great demonstration of knowing that God is in control of everything. We don't know what's best for us but God does. "As the heavens are higher than the earth, so are my ways higher than your ways and my thoughts than your thoughts" (Isaiah 55:9). God's plan is better. His thoughts are higher. We don't need to trust ourselves, we need to trust him.

If you've read much of the Old Testament, you might be familiar with how things worked before Jesus. The sacrifices required to pay for the sins of the people were ugly and would never be enough. When Jesus died on the cross for our sins, this opened up direct access to God. Before Jesus, you couldn't be with God because you were considered not worthy. With Jesus, you now have direct access to God because Jesus is the mediator for you. When he died on the cross, the Bible says the curtain of the temple was torn in two (Matthew 27:51). This symbolizes Jesus bringing us into God's presence. As a believer, his righteousness covers you. You now have access to the father. Amazing, right?

THY WILL BE DONE

Have you ever found yourself making a decision but asking God to bless it? This is different from praying to God and asking him to guide your decision. One says, "My will be done" and the other says, "Thy will be done." These are two very different things. God is not a genie and your prayers are not wishes.

Prayer can be a very private matter between you and God. Jesus often went off on his own to pray. Why did he do that? He did this because he wanted to spend time alone with his father. "But when you pray, go into your room and shut the door and pray to your Father who is in secret. And your Father who sees in secret will reward you" (Matthew 6:6). When we build a relationship with someone, it is both speaking and listening. Prayer is how we talk to God, and reading the Bible is how God talks to us. Are you making time for this in your life? I can't think of a better weapon to take into the battle of fatherhood than the word of God and an active prayer life.

If you want to grow in your prayers, you're in good company. The Bible says, "do not be anxious about anything, but in everything by prayer and supplication with thanksgiving let your requests be made known to God" (Philippians 4:6). To start working on your prayer life, simply start praying more.

Pray when you get up, when you eat, while you're driving, and any other time you think about it. The Bible says to pray without ceasing (1 Thessalonians 5:17). This idea is to always be in fellowship with God. Keep him in all aspects of your life and lean on him through it all.

If you're having trouble getting started, I'll give you a glimpse into my own prayer life. I write down my prayer requests and have them categorized by people and by topic. For my kids, I pray for their faith in God. I pray they would have a desire for the Bible as we read it to them. I pray they will listen to us as they grow up. I ask God to give them good friends to surround them over the years and the courage to push against the world. Since my kids are little, I pray for their salvation, and other things which are specific to their current phase of life.

I typically pray over these requests before I go to bed and I have seen God answer many of them. It's amazing to cross something off a prayer list because it's a reminder of how God cares and is working in our lives. Fathers, I encourage you to start writing down what you want to pray about for your kids.

You can use my examples above but add your own based on their phase of life. There will be many times when you won't know what to do as a father. When you find yourself in one of these moments, pray.

Look for opportunities to model prayer to your children even outside of a routine like meals or bedtime. My daughter Kate was sick with an ear infection over the weekend. She had a particularly high fever which caused us to call the doctor. While my wife was on the phone, I told Titus that we should pray for baby Kate. He prayed, then I prayed. It's in these moments, fathers, that we're building a bridge for our kids to see Jesus. Take every opportunity you get to remind your kids why we pray. You'll start to see their prayer life develop and it's a beautiful thing to watch.

When we picked up Titus from Sunday school recently, his teacher told us a story. She prayed over the class that morning before they started their lesson and when she finished praying, Titus immediately started praying out loud. He did this unprompted in front of the teachers and other kids in the room. He prays with us, and he's not scared to pray with others. Titus is building a bridge for others to see Jesus, even at four years old. I love this story.

I'm thankful he is starting to understand prayer and why we pray. Amy and I have started noticing our daughter Kate (who isn't quite two years old) putting her hands together and bowing her head at dinner when Titus starts to pray. She is watching him and he's teaching her about prayer. There is nothing like being a spectator to God's goodness. Watching the

Holy Spirit move in their life is something we're praying for and we're already starting to see him water their seeds of faith.

Do you keep a prayer list? If not, I've included some blank pages in the back of this book to get you started. You can keep track of prayer requests about your children, other members of your family, friends, coworkers, and even your own personal requests. As you see God answer prayers, come back to this list and cross off the item or add notes to it about how God is working. Watching God move in your life through prayer is powerful and I encourage you to start a list to see how faithful he is in your life.

QUESTIONS FOR FATHERS

1. What are three things you can pray about for your kids?
2. What is a situation in your life that you can pray about as a family?
3. How can you model prayer to your kids at their current age?

PRAYER FOR FATHERS

Pray and ask God to help you make prayer a priority.

10

A FATHER TEACHES

When I found out I was going to have a son, I started thinking about all the fun boy things we could do together. As Titus has grown, I've been counting down the days until I could start teaching him to play baseball. I love baseball. Baseball was my sport, and I enjoyed playing it growing up. I was fortunate to be on the same team for several years with many of my close friends. It was a fun season of life and we still talk about it to this day.

Titus turned four this summer and I thought it was finally time to start working on some fundamentals. I bought him a kid-size t-ball set which included a big orange plastic bat and a hard plastic baseball. At first, he just used it to chase the dog. Shortly after we discouraged this behavior, we made our way into the backyard for our first baseball lesson. I find it challenging as a father to teach my kids anything I've been doing most of my life. What seems like second nature is hard to explain to someone who has never done it before. Let me share an example.

I remember when Titus went from wearing diapers to potty training – it was now my turn to teach him how to go to the bathroom standing up in front of a toilet. A valuable life skill I knew he would appreciate long term. This was an entirely new concept for him and while I tried to explain what he needed to do, he struggled at first with the mechanics. I've been doing this very activity myself for decades and I believe I've got a pretty good handle on it. Although if you ask my wife, there is still room for improvement.

You forget you once had to learn even the simplest of life skills, including going to the bathroom. When you have to describe the process to a three year old, it feels like you're trying to explain quantum physics. I could have had a toilet the size of a kiddie pool but for the first few attempts, he wasn't going to hit it. Thankfully, he's now a pro. Let's get back to baseball.

Once we made it into the backyard, I set up the t-ball set to see if he had any natural ability. He held the wrong end of the bat so I figured now was the time for our first lesson. Once I showed him how to hold the baseball bat, I placed the ball on the tee, and he made contact. I was proud. I was able to watch my son hit a plastic baseball in my backyard. I'm blessed.

Over the summer, Titus started to ask if we could go outside and play baseball after dinner. He didn't have to ask me twice. I didn't hesitate one second and said, "You bet, buddy." We would go outside and start working from the beginning. We worked on holding the bat, squaring up to the plate, and pointing our bat to the sky (a term I coined to teach him to keep his bat up in the air before he swings). I also taught him to have a batting face, which is nothing more than a big smile when I say, "Show me your batting face." It's the best.

After a few weeks, he got the hang of hitting the ball off the tee. I was impressed. He even hit a couple over my head. I decided it was time to make this a little more challenging. Let's see if he can hit the ball when I pitch it to him. I pulled out some beanbags from our cornhole set and placed them in the yard as bases. I showed him how to run around all the bases and back to where he started. This was going to be fun.

All right bud, here it comes. The first few times he was super close to hitting the ball. I was trying hard to put the baseball right in the strike zone making it an easy target. Finally, he got a piece of one and it went pretty far. We celebrated and he wanted to try a few more. Since he's pretty small, I was standing pretty close as I pitched to him. Like most dads, I didn't consider anything could go wrong.

I threw a beautiful pitch right in the sweet spot and he hit it like an MLB player at the home run derby. Before we continue, I want you to remember a time on a show or movie when the scene is paused and someone in the show steps onto the screen to narrate what is about to happen. As soon as Titus connected with the ball, my entire life went into a hyper-slow, out-of-body experience because this hard plastic baseball was headed right for my face. I had absolutely no time to react. I took the ball square to the face and it felt like someone smacked me with a sock full of pennies. For a brief moment, I thought my nose was broken. Thankfully, I was wearing my sunglasses and they absorbed some of the impact.

Immediately, I reached for my nose and all I heard was Titus saying, "Are you ok, dad?" I gently responded, "Good hit, buddy." Amy was standing in silence on the patio with a nervous look as I walked quietly into the house to inspect the damage. After a little while, the redness went away and my nose wasn't broken after all. I made it to the next level as a dad that night; finally, my child was old enough to injure me. We went back out the following night to play again but this time I took a few steps back.

JUST BE TOGETHER

I love teaching my son anything. He's still pretty little and can't do much but I like to include him in whatever I do. When he helps, most jobs take longer than they should but I don't mind. It's fun to see him try to do things that he's too small to attempt. He's helped me change the kitchen faucet, air up the tires on my truck, start the grill for dinner, plant grass seed, clean around the house, assemble furniture, change furnace filters, and many other household tasks.

He usually stands at the bottom of the ladder and hands me tools when I ask. The only issue we have is that he's not a fan of loud noises. Anytime I ask him to help me with something new he points at me and says, "Is it going to make a loud noise?" It's pretty funny.

While I know that Titus isn't able to contribute much at his age, it reminds me of when Jesus started calling his disciples. These guys had all sorts of jobs and knew nothing about being disciples. Jesus didn't care. He simply started teaching them. Little by little, they began to teach others about God, and before too long they were changing the world.

As a father, what are you teaching your children? I think our kids love to learn and I want to encourage you to include them in all activities in life. Take time to teach them about the world around them. Take them on errands, out to dinner, keep them with you when you buy a car, or look at houses. These are all opportunities to share about God and how he's the creator of everything. Teach them to be kind to people they meet when you're out and about. These activities are a way to simply spend time together.

In the Bible, Jesus has the disciples travel around with him and they weren't always doing the most glamorous things. What's incredible to see is as they were eating together, walking together, and traveling together, they were learning about their Heavenly Father. Jesus was constantly teaching them. He is also involving the disciples in many of his miracles. Why is this? He doesn't need their help. He's including them because he wants to teach them about a greater purpose.

In Matthew 14, Jesus feeds 5,000 people using nothing more than five loaves of bread and two fish. Jesus could have fed the crowd in numerous ways but in verse 18, he asks the disciples to bring him the food. Jesus doesn't need this small basket of food. He could just make food out of nothing. He's God. He can do anything. However, it says, "And he directed the people to sit down on the grass. Taking the five loaves and the two fish and looking up to heaven, he gave thanks and broke the loaves. Then he gave them to the disciples, and the disciples gave them to the people" (Matthew 14:19 NIV).

Do you see what Jesus does after he starts to multiply the food? He gives the food to his disciples to have *them* distribute it to the crowd. Jesus is including his disciples in this miracle. He is teaching them how he takes care of the needs of others. He is including them in serving those around him. Jesus is meeting the crowd's immediate need of hunger but at the same time teaching his disciples about a much bigger story. He's teaching them about who he is and what he has come to do.

Stories like this are all over the New Testament. Jesus is being with the disciples, talking to the disciples, and teaching the disciples. As a father, we need to constantly be pouring into our children in the same manner. Jesus takes a group of men who didn't know anything about him. Over time, they started to see who he really was. Jesus was building a bridge which pointed right to him. As Jesus continued to teach them through his ministry, they began to not only follow him but they began to do ministry with him. Jesus sent his disciples all over to heal people and preach the good news. They were going to show others the power of Jesus and how he came to save them.

It was only a few chapters earlier that some of these men were out fishing without any luck. At the time, they didn't know Jesus but now, everything had changed. In Matthew 16:13-14, Jesus asks a question to the disciples, "...'Who do people say that the Son of Man is?' And they said, 'Some say John the

Baptist, others say Elijah, and others Jeremiah or one of the prophets.'"

However, his disciples knew exactly what to think. In verse 15, Jesus asks Peter who he thinks he is. Peter responds, "...'You are the Christ, the Son of the living God.' And Jesus answered him, "Blessed are you, Simon Bar-Jonah! For flesh and blood has not revealed this to you, but my Father who is in heaven'" (Matthew 16:16-17). Peter knew exactly who Jesus was because he had witnessed all the things he had done. He spent time with Jesus each day and learned from him. Jesus taught Peter everything he needed to know over time so he would see who he was.

As fathers, it's this moment we pray for in the lives of our kids. Like the disciples, we get to spend time and help our children grow up. We can choose to be involved or let the world teach them. If we don't teach our children about Jesus, they may not recognize him. However, if we pour into them daily, teach them about God, and pray for the Holy Spirit to move in their life, they may one day walk across the bridge you've been building and say, "I know Jesus."

If you haven't been teaching your kids about Jesus, get started. Don't know where to start? In the chapters ahead we're going to look at a plan you can use with your own family. Start with the small things. Start with prayer. Start today and start pointing them to the perfect father. "And these words that I command you today shall be on your heart. You shall teach them diligently to your children, and shall talk of them when you sit in your house, and when you walk by the way, and when you lie down, and when you rise" (Deuteronomy 6:6-7).

Don't get hung up on what you haven't done. You can't save your kids. Salvation is from the Lord. What a blessing it is to watch your children grow closer to Jesus as they get older. Do what Jesus did for the disciples, teach them about him. "Train up a child in the way he should go; even when he is old he will not depart from it" (Proverbs 22:6).

QUESTIONS FOR FATHERS

1. What specific activity do you remember teaching your children?
2. What are three things you can teach your children about Jesus?
3. How can you include your children in everyday activities?

PRAYER FOR FATHERS

———————————————————————

Pray and ask God to help you teach your children about Jesus.

———————————————————————

11

A FATHER DISCIPLINES

"License and registration, please." This is the phrase no one wants to hear. I sat in silence. What am I going to do? Maybe I can get out of this. Maybe I can talk my way out. Nope, he's pulling out his pen. This isn't going to be good...

The summer before high school and college was a fun season of life. I had just returned from a mission trip and was headed to college in the fall. However, there was one surprise ahead that would make my summer even better.

SPEED LIMITS

Like most teenage boys, I've always enjoyed cars. I was lucky and my parents surprised me with a Mustang before I headed off to school. This car was awesome. It was black with a leather interior and had a 5-speed manual transmission. The V8 engine sounded amazing. It had a very retro look and every time I would hop inside, it felt like I was driving it for the first time.

I remember getting into my car one afternoon to head over to a friend's house. It was a nice summer day outside and the sun was shining. I was driving down a road in the middle of our town when all of a sudden, I saw a police car hidden off on a side street. I did what most people do, I quickly tapped my brakes and didn't even look to see how fast I was going. Suddenly, I saw red and blue lights turn on and the police car pulled out behind me. I pulled over in silence. I was nervous as I awaited the officer at my door. I rolled down my window and he said, "License and registration, please." "Sure, no problem." I was hoping he was a fellow car enthusiast but by the look on his face, he seemed like he wasn't enthused about much right now.

The street I was driving on was one of those streets that had a speed limit from the 1800s, when people rode horses everywhere. You know what I mean, right? I'm still trying to justify this to myself after all these years. He looked at my license and asked, "Do you know how fast you were going?" I nervously responded, "Um, no. I don't." Wrong answer.

"I clocked you going 44 in a 30." I thought about asking him if he also felt this street should have a higher speed limit, but he didn't seem interested in debating this topic. He headed back to his patrol car and I felt like a prisoner waiting for execution. I thought to myself that maybe he wouldn't give me a ticket. Then I reminded myself of what I'm driving. I thought, "How excited is he going to be to give the young kid with the mustang a ticket today?" I'm not feeling very good about this one.

I see him get out of his patrol car and start walking back to mine. He's holding one of those carbon copy pieces of paper where you tear off the edge and each person keeps a piece. This isn't looking good. He got to my window and said, "Here's your ticket." I was crushed. I had just received my first speeding ticket in the vehicle my parents had just purchased for me and I couldn't think of how this could get any worse. However, it did, thanks to my stupidity.

Three weeks later almost to the day, I'm driving a few blocks away from where I got my speeding ticket. All of a sudden, I passed a police car and saw those familiar red and blue lights. It was at this moment that I thought I was dreaming. Is this really happening, again? I remember pulling over and when the officer got out, I turned ghost white. It was the same officer from three weeks ago. Will he remember me? What is he going to do? Should I try to make small talk? What if I tell him I remember him from three weeks ago? Ok, the last one was a bad idea.

"License and registration, please." I was able to provide these a little faster this time since it was becoming a common occurrence in my life. He walked back to his patrol car without saying another word. He didn't stay there long. I see him get out and walk towards me with the same carbon copy-style paper. I'm dead.

Before we go any further, I would just like to point out two things. First, this is my fault. Both times. I have no one to blame but myself. Second, why is this street only 30 MPH? I was able to get some grace from my parents on the first ticket but I don't think the second one will be as easy.

When I got home and told my parents that I got my second speeding ticket in one month, they weren't pleased. I deserved to be punished as it was embarrassing and a lack of better judgment on my part. Getting disciplined is hard but giving discipline is hard, too. As a father, I hate to punish my kids but I love them. It would be unloving of me to not discipline my children.

DISCIPLINE IS LOVING

Why do we hate discipline? Have you ever thought about this? Why do we fear getting into trouble? Like several examples in this book, it goes back to the beginning. When Adam and Eve first sinned, it messed up everything. Up to this point, they were both naked and not ashamed (Genesis 2:25). They were in full fellowship with God and enjoyed being in his presence. Once they sinned, everything changed. As soon as they ate of the tree, they realized they were naked and scripture says, "Then the eyes of both were opened, and they knew that they were naked. And they sewed fig leaves together and made themselves loincloths" (Genesis 3:7). Realizing they were naked was a representation of broken fellowship with God. They were now in opposition to him.

The following verse shows how we all feel about discipline in our life. "And they heard the sound of the LORD God walking in the garden in the cool of the day, and the man and his wife hid themselves from the presence of the LORD God among the trees of the garden" (Genesis 3:8). Both Adam and

Eve were hiding from God because they knew they were in trouble. They didn't want to face their creator and Heavenly Father. This is the same feeling that I had when I saw the officer carrying the speeding tickets back to my car. I knew my parents were going to be mad and all I wanted to do was hide.

GOD IS HOLY

Why should God discipline Adam and Eve? Why should he discipline us? This is paramount to the entire Bible. First, God is good. He is only good. He is nothing but good. His entire nature is good. Therefore, God can only be around those who are also good. Up until this point, Adam and Eve were sinless and were able to be in fellowship with God. Now, they weren't.

Second, God is Holy. The Hebrew word for Holy means *set apart*. By being set apart, God can't be around sin. Sin is the opposite of God's nature and everything he is about. To give you a little perspective on how Holy our God is, let's look at the ark of the covenant and tabernacle. In the Old Testament, the ark of the covenant was a gold-plated wooden box that God asked the Israelites to build which housed the ten commandments. It would sit in the Most Holy place, which was the innermost room of the tabernacle. The room was separated by a huge curtain and only the high priest could enter this room once a year after atoning for his sins. God's presence would hover over the ark and everyone else would have to stay outside.

Once a year, the high priest would enter the Most Holy place in the tabernacle. If the priest didn't atone for his sins properly, he would die when he entered the room. Tradition holds that they would tie a rope around the high priest with bells so if he died, they would hear the bells and could drag his body out of the tabernacle.

Another example representing God's holiness was how the ark was required to be moved. The ark was required to be carried on two long poles. There is a story in 2 Samuel where some men are moving the ark but instead of carrying it as God required, it was being moved on a cart. The oxen pulling the cart stumbled and Uzzah reached out and touched the ark to catch it. He was struck dead for his deed.

If you think this might be harsh, remember God is Holy. His holiness cannot be with sin. God gave clear instructions on how to transport the ark and the group failed to follow through. If God doesn't hold us accountable then he isn't good. Which as we've seen, would be clearly against his nature. A good father disciplines his children just like God disciplines us. When we are disciplined, it's to help us understand how we need to turn from sin and follow him. If God didn't discipline us, we wouldn't seek God. Discipline is good. It's loving and as we'll see, not disciplining your children is one of the worst things you can do as a father.

God doesn't force us to love him. He gives all of us free will. After Adam and Eve sinned, things were going to change. God told them in Genesis that some of the things they took for granted would no longer be easy. For example, Adam was going to toil at work to produce food from the ground and Eve was going to have pain during childbirth. In addition, God could have killed them or even started over. He could have left them in their sin without any hope. Our God is a good father and while he did discipline his children for their actions, he immediately reached out to help.

"And the LORD God made for Adam and for his wife garments of skins and clothed them" (Genesis 3:21). God knew they were now naked and ashamed, but instead of leaving them in their broken state, he made clothes for them to take care of them. This would be a picture of how God would later give Jesus to cover our sins. God would have been perfectly within his right to kill off Adam and Eve. He's God. He can do whatever he wants to do. While this would have been fair, our God doesn't give us what we deserve. If he did, we would all be destined for Hell without any hope. We know this isn't how the story ends. God provides Jesus so that we can have our sins covered once and for all. Our fellowship with God can be restored if we trust in him.

"There is therefore now no condemnation for those who are in Christ Jesus" (Romans 8:1). This verse represents how we don't get what we deserve. If you're a follower of Jesus, you don't have to fear God's wrath. Jesus has taken the punishment you deserved and God is satisfied. God's discipline is for our benefit because he loves us and has our best interests at heart.

This is the same way we should feel about our children. I want the best for Titus and Kate. I want them to have a life where they understand God's plan. I want to protect them from bad things and I will be happy to discipline them along the way because I love them. "Whoever spares the rod hates his son, but he who loves him is diligent to discipline him" (Proverbs 13:24). Anytime I have to discipline my children, it hurts, but it doesn't hurt as much as watching them live in sin. Sin is destructive and harmful. Sin leads to death. If I don't correct my children but instead let them continue in their sins, I'm not a good father and neither are you.

DISCIPLINE IS HARD

There will be times when you are also on the end of God's discipline. When this happens, how will you respond? The Bible says, "My son, do not despise the LORD's discipline or be weary of his reproof, for the LORD reproves him whom he loves, as a father the son in whom he delights" (Proverbs 3:11-12). If you find yourself amid God's discipline, you're loved. While it may be a hard season, you're being drawn to the perfect father because he can't stand to see his children in sin.

Our God is patient and slow to anger. He is always watching over us and helping us in times of trouble. Raising children isn't easy; it's very hard. As fathers, we won't always make the right decisions when it comes to discipline, but in order to love our children well, we must learn to discipline, too.

I want to be a father who disciplines his children, but I also want to be a father that my children can run in times of trouble. I don't want to be a father who is feared. It's easy to lose our heads when our children make mistakes, especially ones with earthly consequences. However, if we can learn to be patient and slow to anger as our perfect father treats us, we'll build yet another bridge to Jesus.

QUESTIONS FOR FATHERS

1. What makes disciplining your children difficult?
2. What areas of your children's life need discipline?
3. How can you show love during a moment of discipline?

PRAYER FOR FATHERS

Pray and ask God to help you discipline your children as a reflection of your love.

12

A FATHER GIVES

I love to give my children gifts. I'm always waiting for the moment I can finally reveal what we've been hiding from them. As a father, you're all too familiar with putting together toys late into the night. Perhaps you have a story where you spent Christmas Eve putting together a bike or play set just so your kids could see it all together on Christmas morning.

When Titus and Kate were born, I found myself wanting to run out and get them fun toys they would enjoy. I would often get ahead of myself and purchase something well before they were ready for it. When Titus turned two years old, I was determined to get him a Jeep to ride around in our backyard. He was barely able to walk, but for some reason, I was set on surprising him so he could cruise around. I did some research online and purchased one which came with a cheap remote control for the parents to operate. I figured since he likely wouldn't be able to drive it, I could drive him around myself.

When it arrived, there were two issues that I was going to have to overcome. First, I needed to put it together. Thankfully, it came mostly assembled but I needed to attach the wheels and charge the battery. Second, I needed some place to hide it. Most toys, up to this point in his life, were able to be secretly tucked away in the basement closet or another room in our home. This battery-powered Jeep wasn't going to be so easy to hide. Once I got it assembled, I covered it with a sheet in our garage. For the next few weeks, I tried to avoid this area when we would go to and from the house. I was hoping his little curiosity wouldn't lead him right to his birthday surprise.

Finally, the day had come and it was all I could think about. I remember rushing through lunch to prepare for the grand reveal. I walked into the garage and wheeled this thing around to the backyard. I attached some balloons to it and gathered our family who were over to celebrate. His face lit up immediately and he ran over to it and climbed in. I pushed the button to turn it on and held the remote control in my hands. He was ready to set off across the yard. As I drove him around the backyard he had the biggest smile on his face. As a father, I enjoyed every moment. He was still very little and it would be a couple of years until could drive it on his own, but for this moment, I was so excited to give him this gift.

I believe God loves to give his children gifts, just like we love to give gifts to our children. When Titus was riding around our yard, he didn't have anything to do with *getting* the gift. The Jeep we got Titus was a one-way gift. He didn't pay for it. He didn't earn it. He didn't even ask for it. However, I love Titus and I wanted to do something special for him.

What is the definition of a gift? A gift is something given to you without payment or anything given in return. It's completely out of love from the giver. Your life is a gift from God. Everything we have discussed in the book is a reflection of how God is the ultimate giver. The Bible says, "For by grace you have been saved through faith. And this is not your own doing; it is the gift of God" (Ephesians 2:8). This verse represents how, through God's grace, we have been saved if we have put our faith in Jesus. There was nothing we could have done to earn the gift of Jesus. There is nothing Titus could have worked for to buy the Jeep. It was completely out of his reach. While this analogy falls short of how wonderful the gift of salvation is to you and me, it's a small reminder of how our God loves us.

In this book, we've learned how God gives us everything. He doesn't hold back. He provides and protects us. He serves and helps us in times of trouble. He listens to us when we pray. He teaches us about him and how we should live. He disciplines us when we go astray and he gives without any form of selfishness. Above everything, he's given us the ultimate gift in Jesus. He's the perfect father and our model for fatherhood.

What gifts has God given you? What about today? How about life itself? This may not be something you stop to consider but by waking up today, you've been given a gift. God has you alive for a purpose. Each morning and every heartbeat is a gift from our creator. Not only is he the source of life, but he's also the sustainer of it. "This is the day that the LORD has made; let us rejoice and be glad in it" (Psalm 118:24). Every night when you get in bed, take a moment to thank God for the gift of today.

As fathers, our children frequently ask us to give our time to them. They may want us to play with them or help them with a task. How do you handle these requests? Do you say, "Not right now" or "Maybe later." At times these are appropriate responses but is this how our Heavenly Father treats us? When you pray to God does he say, "I'm busy right now" or "Come back in 30 minutes"? No, he always listens and is ready to help his children. He gives his time to us because he loves us. Are you a father who gives your time to your kids?

There are times after a long day of work when Titus and Kate ask me to "fly" them around the living room. I'm exhausted and there have been times when I've said no. However, I've tried recently to take a breath and say, "Yes, I'll fly you around the living room." They scream in excitement and off we go. This simple response isn't me being a perfect dad; I can't be. It is a reminder to me to look at my Heavenly Father because this is how he treats me.

Have you taken a moment recently to think about what else God has given you? What about rest? Rest is critical as a father. What does this mean to rest? Does it mean to sleep? We know as a father there will be many sleepless nights. Jesus says, "Come to me, all who labor and are heavy laden, and I will give you rest. Take my yoke upon you, and learn from me, for I am gentle and lowly in heart, and you will find rest for your souls. For my yoke is easy, and my burden is light" (Matthew 11:28-30). The rest Jesus is describing is peace. When we rest in him, we have the comfort to get through anything.

As a father, are you resting in him? The verse above describes a yoke. A yoke is a wooden beam that two animals, typically oxen, would have around their necks which help them pull very heavy loads. Isn't life heavy at times? Don't you often feel the stress of the day? Are there things that keep you up at night? As fathers, how will we get through it all? How will we navigate the journey we discussed throughout this book? If we try to pull the heavy load of life on our own, it's going to be hard. However, if we take the yoke Jesus has offered us, the burden will be light. He will get us through it all.

Jesus is offering us help and he's yet offering us another gift. In the verse above Jesus is offering for you to place all of your problems as a father on him. He wants to lead your life and he wants you to point your children to him. God's rest is better than any good night's sleep. It's his rest that allows us to sleep well knowing he's in control. Are you resting in him today?

Thankfully, our kids have always been good sleepers. As every parent knows, the first several weeks with a newborn baby can be challenging for many reasons but sleep is at the top of the list. After these initial weeks, our children got into a routine and we're grateful that they have stayed with it. Only recently have our nights started to be interrupted while we sleep.

Lately, Titus has started getting out of his bed and walking to our room in the middle of the night. At first, this was very unusual for us all. We would walk him back to his room and he would go back to sleep. Some nights this happens once, others a couple of times. Occasionally, we get through an entire night without him waking us up. Since he's always been good at sleeping through the night, I know this recent change is only a phase as he gets older. He's started to become more fearful at night when he wakes up and this has caused him to seek us out for reassurance that everything is ok. There is a similar story in the Bible where the disciples went to Jesus when they were scared. He was also sleeping. Let's take a look at this passage and see how a father gives of himself even when he's exhausted.

THE STORMS OF LIFE

In Matthew chapter 8, we see Jesus and his disciples get into a boat. While they're all out on the water, a large storm arose. It says the storm was even causing waves to come over the boat. They are all very frightened. Several of the disciples had been fishermen in the past so it wasn't the first time they had encountered a storm. However, this one was particularly severe.

During the storm, Jesus was sleeping (Matthew 8:24). What I like about this verse is while the disciples are scared and stressed out, Jesus is resting on the same boat. Jesus is resting because he is trusting his father. He's at peace during the storm. He's able to sleep during a rough time. "The disciples went and woke him, saying, 'Lord, save us! We're going to drown!" (Matthew 8:25 NIV).

They were scared and they feared they would die. At this moment Jesus could have said, "Guys, I'm tired. I've been healing people and traveling quite a bit lately. I just want to get some sleep. Can you all deal with your problems on your own for once? I'm going back to bed." However, Jesus gets up and gives the disciples his attention and love. He put their needs above his own and gave of himself at this moment. "He replied,

'You of little faith, why are you so afraid?' Then he got up and rebuked the winds and the waves, and it was completely calm" (Matthew 8:26 NIV).

Like a good father, Jesus got up and helped. Jesus has control over the storm because he has control over everything. When our children come to us amid a storm in their life, how will we respond? There are going to be many storms in life. Some we will face ourselves, and others will be storms our children will face. However, who are we looking at during the storm? We can always go "wake Jesus." He's ready to give us his help.

The Bible says, "For everyone who asks receives, and the one who seeks finds, and to the one who knocks it will be opened. Or which one of you, if his son asks him for bread, will give him a stone? Or if he asks for a fish, will give him a serpent? If you then, who are evil, know how to give good gifts to your children, how much more will your Father who is in heaven give good things to those who ask him!" (Matthew 7:8-11). As fathers, we know how to give gifts to our children so why are we not asking our Heavenly Father more often for good things in our life?

God knows what we need and like a good father, he may not give us what we ask for because it's not best for us. Remember, "Every good gift and every perfect gift is from above, coming down from the Father of lights, with whom there is no variation or shadow due to change" (James 1:17). As a father, be a giver. Give your time, give your strength, give your love, give your money, give your energy. Give your all to your children because you're Heavenly Father gave it all for you.

QUESTIONS FOR FATHERS

1. How can you be a giving father to your children this week?
2. What is the hardest area of your life to give?
3. How can you teach your children to be givers like Jesus?

PRAYER FOR FATHERS

Pray and ask God to help you have a giving heart.

13

KNOWING THE FATHER

You're going to die. Someday, it will happen. It might be years away or it might be tomorrow. I know that's some bad news to hear but keep reading and I promise we'll talk about some good news, too. I'm sure you're thinking that's a fairly harsh way to start this chapter, but unfortunately, it's the truth. No person in the world is excluded from this reality. Have you ever stopped to think about how death affects every single person in the world? No matter where you grow up or what language you speak, death is inevitable.

Why is death still a part of life after all the advancements in the world? What happens after you die? Throughout this book, we have referenced the Bible to see how God has displayed to us the ultimate picture of fatherhood. However, the Bible tells us about much more than fatherhood. If what we've learned about Jesus throughout this book has spoken to you, then this chapter is for you.

Perhaps our discussion of sin and death is something you haven't thought about much. What about Jesus? I'm sure you've heard about him. Do you remember in chapter six when we discussed how Jesus asked Peter who he was? What if Jesus asked you the same question? What would you say?

I want to bring us back to the first statement in this chapter. It's the idea of death. I don't like to think about death. It's ugly. I hope it's decades away but I have no control over it and neither do you. Since we live in a world where death exists, there is another question to ponder. Where did we come from? How did we get here? What do you think?

I'm sure you've heard various theories throughout your life but if you had to bet on one, what would it be? If someone asked you how we got here, what would you say? Take a moment to walk over to a window as you think about this question. Look out and take in all that you see. You'll probably see trees, birds, the sky, perhaps other people walking around, and other signs of life. Where did all of this come from?

You could ask any number of people their opinion but if you ask me, I would point you to the same source we've used throughout this book. I'm going to point you to the Bible. Let's see what it has to say on this topic. The very first verse in the entire Bible can answer this question for you. While the Bible is a rather large book, you don't have to search for how you got here. All you need to do is read the beginning of the first page. It says, "In the beginning, God created the heavens and the earth" (Genesis 1:1). This is foundational to everything else. God has always existed. This is a hard concept to understand but if you can rest in this reality, you'll understand how it all fits together.

God created everything. Yes, everything. He created the sun, moon, stars, earth, people, food, animals, plants, and anything else you can list out. He is the source of life. He is the creator. This is why we refer to him as *God the father*. He is the beginning of everything that has ever been created. If you remember earlier in this book, we talked about Adam and Eve. God created them. He loved creating them and they reflected his image. They were in fellowship with God in the Garden of Eden and had everything that God created at their disposal.

Do you remember when we discussed that God is good? Let's do a quick recap of this. God is only good. His nature by definition is good, and because he is good, he cannot be with sin. If you remember, sin is anything against God's nature. It's the opposite of his character and goes against everything he is. When Adam and Eve sinned in the garden, their sin separated them from God. The fellowship they once had was now broken.

The Bible says, "Therefore, just as sin came into the world through one man, and death through sin, and so death spread to all men because all sinned" (Romans 5:12). If you have ever wondered why death occurs, it's because of sin. This verse tells us that through the sin of Adam, sin spread to all people going forward. Every person on this earth is in the lineage of Adam and Eve. They were the first humans God created. Since Adam sinned, death was now going to be a part of our world. Now everyone in the world is going to die because we are all sinners.

Not only are you a sinner as a descendant of Adam, but you

have sinned, too. Ever told a lie? That's a sin. Ever been jealous of something someone has? That's called coveting and it's sin. Ever looked at another person with a lustful desire? You guessed it – sin. We could name several more sinful behaviors but just know, you're guilty of sin. All of the above are against God's good nature.

The idea of being a sinner might sound judgmental. You might be thinking, "I'm not a bad person." The idea of being a *good* or *bad* person is not something you or I get to decide. Why? It's because we're not God. He is the one who gets to decide. Another verse describing this reality is, "for all have sinned and fall short of the glory of God" (Romans 3:23). Again, we see it says "all" which means everyone. This is you, me, and everyone in the world. No one is excluded.

If you'll notice, this verse talks about "the glory of God." What does it mean to "fall short." Not only is God good, but he is also perfect. Since he's perfect, the standard is perfection. If you aren't perfect, you can't meet the standard. Now I'm guessing you're starting to see how being a good person isn't good enough according to the Bible.

Ok, here's some more bad news. Not only will you die but you won't be able to spend eternity with God in Heaven because of your sinful nature. This is bad news. The alternative to Heaven is Hell. People don't like to talk about Hell. Some people like to think only about Heaven. However, the same Bible that talks about Heaven also talks about Hell. The reality of Hell is an eternity separated from God. Most people think *good* people go to heaven, but as we've just seen, this isn't the case because no one is good.

So after hearing all of this bad news, I've got the best news that you'll ever hear; since you or I couldn't get to God on our own, God, in his infinite love, came to us. Yes, the God of the universe reached out to help because there was no hope for any of us. We needed a sacrifice to pay for our sins. Since God is holy, there must be a payment for our sinful nature. Ready for the good news? Ok, here it is – it's Jesus.

The person we've discussed the most in this book is the best news you've ever going to hear. In the Bible, Jesus says, "...I am the way, and the truth, and the life. No one comes to the Father except through me" (John 14:6). God sent Jesus to die on the cross for our sins. Jesus lived a perfect life and paid the debt we all owed. Not only did Jesus come and die, but he also did it for a bunch of people who didn't love him. The Bible says, "but God shows his love for us in that while we were still sinners, Christ died for us" (Romans 5:8).

Almost everyone in the world *knows about* Jesus but not everyone *knows* Jesus. These are completely different. Let me give you an example. I know about the President of the United States but I don't personally know the President. See what I mean? You've likely been exposed to Jesus or the idea of him throughout your life. Let's see what Jesus has to say about himself. He says, "...Whoever has seen me has seen the Father..." (John 14:9). He also says, "I and the Father are one" (John 10:30). To know Jesus is to know the father. How so, you might ask? Jesus is God!

Jesus dying on the cross allows us to have fellowship again with God. It makes everything that was broken by sin whole again. Knowing Jesus is how we can be forgiven of our sins.

Knowing about Jesus won't save us from anything. See the difference? The Bible says, "For the wages of sin is death, but the free gift of God is eternal life in Christ Jesus our Lord" (Romans 6:23). You can't do anything to earn salvation on your own. You have to put your faith in Jesus.

Every other religion in the world is based on works. What can *you do* to earn salvation? Well, according to the Bible, nothing. You can't *do* anything. This is why God sent Jesus. Everyone is trying to earn salvation and it won't get you anywhere. God is offering a gift to you in Jesus to pay for your sins and give you eternal life. The life he is offering doesn't start once you die, it starts the moment you let him into your life. This is great news!

It doesn't matter what you've done. It doesn't matter your past. It doesn't matter if you're eight years old or eighty-eight. Jesus is hoping you'll trust him for your salvation. How do you do this? It's simple. The Bible says, "...everyone who calls on the name of the Lord will be saved" (Romans 10:13). Pray to God, admitting you're a sinner in need of Jesus. Pray to him confessing your sins, ask for forgiveness, and for Jesus to be your Lord. The Bible says, "...if you confess with your mouth that Jesus is Lord and believe in your heart that God raised him from the dead, you will be saved" (Romans 10:9). While Jesus died on the cross, he didn't stay dead. Three days later, God raised him from the dead. Death doesn't have a hold on him. He beat death and he did it for you. The resurrection of Jesus is the most wonderful event that has ever happened. His resurrection brings salvation to us all.

You don't have to know everything about the Bible. You

don't have to get right before you come to God. You just have to realize you can't save yourself, and instead, come to Jesus. That's it. It's all about what he did and not what you've done. You have to move from a reliance on yourself to a reliance on him. If you put your faith in Jesus, you'll be justified in God's eyes. It will be just as if you've never sinned. The Bible says, "There is therefore now no condemnation for those who are in Christ Jesus" (Romans 8:1).

Jesus has changed me. He's changed everything. I could write an entire book on how he has personally saved me and changed my life. He is my Lord and I want him to be yours, too. Life is hard. The world is confusing but I'm thankful I have a savior who helps me through the ups and downs of it all.

The Bible says, "Enter by the narrow gate. For the gate is wide and the way is easy that leads to destruction, and those who enter by it are many. For the gate is narrow and the way is hard that leads to life, and those who find it are few" (Matthew 7:13-14). Here's the reality. Most people won't choose Jesus. Most people will decide they want to be their own savior. Most people will decide they want to seek after the things of the world. Most people will miss the truth in scripture. Will you?

Throughout the book, we talked about the decision of being a father. If you've put your faith in Jesus, reflect on what he has done for you and thank him for saving you. If you've never put your faith in Jesus, you have one more decision to make. It's time for you to respond to the same question he asked Peter. You've seen the world and all it has to offer. You understand death is a guarantee. You can look out the window and know all of this was created by someone. You can come up with your own theory or you can trust the Bible. You can rely on yourself or put your faith in him. Jesus is asking you, "Who do you say I am?" You now have the decision to make. What will you say?

14

THE FRAMEWORK

While our journey in this book is coming to a close, your fatherhood journey is not. It doesn't matter if you're a father who is twenty-three or a grandfather who is ninety-three. If you're alive, you're on a mission. God's design for fathers is the same today as it has been from the beginning. Your role is to love and shepherd your household by pointing your family to Jesus.

As you've read this book, you've seen a picture of who God is as a father to us and how he wants us to demonstrate fatherhood to our children. You learned the true meaning of a father and the responsibilities God designed you for as a man. You've learned about who you were as the "old man" before you came to know Jesus, and who you are now as the new man in him.

So, now what? Now is the moment when you're at a fork in the road. You can go in one of two directions. You can choose to be the father God designed you to be or you can choose to be the father who sits back and hopes their children will be ok on their own. My prayer for you is you'll be the first father – the one who stands up in our world to serve their household well and teaches other men to do the same. If your children are little, get in the game now, don't waste another moment. If your children are adults, be involved in their life any way you can. Love, serve, pray, shepherd, and point them to Jesus. You can do it!

If you're ready for a tangible step or something which you can implement with your household today, I'm going to walk you through a framework I think you'll enjoy. I've put together a plan for fathers to walk through with their own families using what we have discussed in this book. This is a plan designed to draw your family closer together and closer to Jesus.

You might have a personal quiet time each day, or you might even be in a small group at church, but it's unlikely you are currently setting aside time together each week as a family to study God's word in your very own home. Fathers, if you're ready for the next step, let's get started.

PICK A TIME

It is crucial you spend time with your family together in the Bible. First, you're going to need to set aside thirty minutes each week together. This could be a weeknight or the weekend. Make sure to plan when everyone can attend. This is especially critical if your children are older and have sports or other activities which take their time.

Once you have this time established, put it on the calendar.

This may be a shared calendar on everyone's phones or a written calendar on the fridge. The idea is for everyone to know you have a set time each week when you're going to spend time together as a family reading the Bible.

STEP ONE - OPENING PRAYER (FATHER)

Each time you meet, pause and pray for the time you'll spend in God's word. As the father, I encourage you to be the one who opens your time together in prayer each week. I think this is a good way to symbolize how God designed you to be responsible for your household and it reminds you personally of your duty. You don't have to have a long prayer or say anything specific. Just thank God for your family and the opportunity to spend time together right now. Ask the Holy Spirit to teach you as you read the passage of the week and guide your hearts towards him. There will be an opportunity later on for prayer requests and praises, but this moment should just be a prayer to get the night started.

STEP TWO - READ THE OVERVIEW

Start by reading the overview of this week's story out loud so everyone can understand the passage you're about to read. If your children are old enough, have everyone take notes. We want to hear what the Bible has to say, but we also want to study it. Write down anything that sticks out to you or even things that you're not sure of their meaning. This is a great way to build discussion points as we move through the passage in scripture.

STEP THREE - READ THE STORY

Each week, you're going to read a story from the Bible. Use a real Bible and not your phone. This should be a phone-free time as a family. Have everyone put the phones away so there are no distractions. If your children are old enough, take turns reading the story each week. It's a great way to get everyone involved while spending time together.

Each week, you'll focus on a characteristic of God which reflects his fatherhood to all of us along with a Bible story and questions to discuss together. I've taken the characteristics we've discussed in the book and designed a way for you to study them with your family. You'll look at God's love, provision, forgiveness, and protection. You'll see how he serves, helps, and teaches us to pray. You'll discuss how he is the ultimate giver by giving us Jesus.

STEP FOUR - DISCUSSION QUESTIONS

Each week, I've included a series of questions related to the story. The questions will take up the most time because everyone will contribute. Don't rush this part of your time together. Allow plenty of time once you read the questions for everyone to gather their thoughts. It takes some people longer than others before they're ready to share and this is ok. Feel free to answer the questions as each person is ready or go around in a circle for your discussion giving everyone a chance to speak.

STEP FIVE - VERSE OF THE WEEK

At the end of the story, you'll have a verse for the week. If you have a chalkboard or another place to display it in your home, that is a great place to write the verse. I encourage each person to memorize the verse and recite it when they meet the following week. Challenge each other to memorize the verse throughout the week. Randomly ask each other to recite it and see who can do it. Fathers, set the example and be the first one to recite it each week.

STEP SIX - CLOSING PRAYER

Before you end your time together, go around and take prayer requests. Make sure to write these down. Put them somewhere where everyone can see them. You'll want to write them down for a couple of reasons. First, you want everyone to be able to see the list so they can pray over these items throughout the week. It's also a great time to discuss and write down praises. These are moments you can celebrate together as a family. These can be for the healing of someone in your life or even a personal achievement that took place.

Second, you'll want to keep this list around so each week you can add to it and cross things off as you see God answer prayers. This should be a living list as it will change over time. Finally, once you have discussed everyone's prayer and praise requests, have someone pray to close out the time together. Take turns each week or even split up the list so everyone can pray over a couple of items.

FRAMEWORK SUMMARY

Spending time together as a family to read, pray, and love one another is life-changing. Don't take the time you have for granted. I believe once your children are grown, they will look back on this time spent together as something they cherished. It will draw everyone closer together and more importantly, closer to Jesus.

To help you get started, I've created an eight-week family devotional using this framework. If you don't currently have a plan in place with your family, I encourage you to check it out. I've included a QR code at the back of this book you can scan with your phone to download The Fatherhood Framework Family Plan. It's a great way to help get you started growing together.

MEN'S STUDY GUIDE

If you're interested in leading other men through The Fatherhood Framework material, I've put together a study guide for your church, small group, or Bible study. The Fatherhood Framework Study Guide will help equip you and other men to be the fathers, husbands, and leaders that God designed you to be. It provides a comprehensive walkthrough of The Fatherhood Framework book with instructions and practical guidance to grow as fathers going forward. You can learn more about the study guide in the pages ahead.

CONCLUSION

I wanted to let you know you inspire me. By reading this book you're interested in becoming a better father, too. We need this now more than ever. I'm not perfect and neither are you. We're going to mess up and some days will be hard but we're on this journey together. Hang in there, fight the good fight, and with Jesus, we'll be just fine. You can do this. No matter what you do, keep your eyes on the perfect father. As you close this book you now have a decision to make. What kind of father will you be? "But as for me and my house, we will serve the LORD." (Joshua 25:15). I've made my choice. What will you do?

THANK YOU

Would you do me a favor? If you enjoyed this book, would you take a moment to leave a review on Amazon? I would love to read how this book encouraged you in your fatherhood journey. It will also help this book gain more exposure to other readers looking for material on fatherhood.

Scan the QR code below to leave a review.

SHARE THIS BOOK

Do you think others should read The Fatherhood Framework? Take a photo holding the book and post it online encouraging others to check it out. #thefatherhoodframework

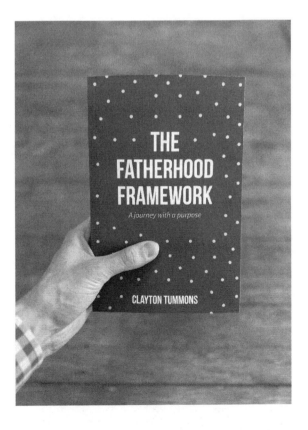

FAMILY PLAN

The Fatherhood Framework Family Plan is an eight-week devotional designed to draw your family closer together and closer to Jesus. Each week, you'll focus on a characteristic of God which reflects his fatherhood to all of us along with a Bible story and questions to discuss together.

The material is appropriate for all ages, so whether your children are young or in their teenage years, you'll find applications for everyone. It all starts with fathers leading their households, and this plan is a fantastic guide to help you along the way.

Scan the QR code below to download the family plan.

STUDY GUIDE

The Fatherhood Framework Study Guide is perfect for your church, small group, Bible study, or just yourself. The curriculum will help equip you and other men to be the fathers, husbands, and leaders that God designed you to be. This program provides a comprehensive walkthrough of The Fatherhood Framework book with instructions and practical guidance to grow as fathers going forward.

Fathers are meant for more, and I believe equipping men with this calling will help point them, their families, and others to Jesus. If you're interested in leading other men through The Fatherhood Framework material, this study is a great plan to guide you along the way.

Scan the QR code below for the study guide.

ABOUT THE AUTHOR

Clayton Tummons is a father living in the Midwest. He's blessed to be married to his wife Amy and has two wonderful children. He spends his free time with family, church, fitness, playing guitar, and is passionate about teaching others about Jesus.

NOTES

1. What is a Father?

1. U.S. Census Bureau. (2015). C3. Living arrangements of children under 18 years/1 and marital status of parents, by age, sex,
    race, and hispanic origin/2 and selected characteristics of the child for all children: 2012. Washington, D.C. U.S. Census Bureau.
2. U.S. Department of Health and Human Services. National Center for Health Statistics. Survey on Child Health. Washington, DC, 1993.
3. SOURCE: Pougnet, E., Serbin, L. A., Stack, D. M., Ledingham, J. E., & Schwartzman, A. E. (2012). The intergenerational continuity of
    fathers' absence in a socioeconomically disadvantaged sample, Journal of Marriage and
    Family, 74(3), 540-555.
4. James, Doris J. Profile of Jail Inmates, 2002. (NCJ 201932). Bureau of Justice Statistics Special Report, Department of Justice, Office of Justice Programs, July 2004.

PRAYER LIST

Made in the USA
Monee, IL
16 May 2024